# GENERATIONAL

# CURSES

# &

# THE BELIEVER

**Busuyi Aroso**

PUBLISHED BY
KRATOS PUBLISHER

# DEDICATION

I dedicate this book to Yomi, my lovely wife with whom

I serve God. I also dedicate this book to Tomi & Toni,

my beautiful daughters who continue to support

me in the work of the ministry.

# Contents

# INTRODUCTION

The decision to write this book became important to me after attending some meetings where the supposedly Bible-trained and knowledgeable people, some of whom attended what can be described as "Elite Charismatic Bible Schools", who should know better, said things about "Generational Curses" relative to the believer that are outrightly unbiblical.

Even though I have known all along that some Christians in some quarters hold some erroneous beliefs about the subject of generational curses, I didn't realise how widespread it has become. My expectation for this book is to shed the light of God's Word on the subject, trusting that my brothers and sisters in the Body of Christ will be humble enough to let God's Spirit guide us to all truth regarding the issue of generational curses.

The Bible makes it unequivocally clear that redemption from curses was part of the finished work of Jesus Christ through his crucifixion, death and resurrection. It is also clear that anyone who has been born again has been redeemed from all curses. Unfortunately, some still go around telling New Covenant believers that they are subject to the so-called generational curses. They say that believers will not be able to live victorious in Christ unless generational curses are broken off their lives. Friends, this is not consistent with the truth of the Bible.

The phrase "generational curses" does not exist anywhere in the Bible. It is sometimes difficult to understand what people mean when they use terminologies not found in the Bible. The only way to understand what Christians who talk about generational curses mean is to listen to their examples and explanations that define the concept.

My purpose for writing this book is not to be controversial but like I mentioned earlier, is to shed light on God's word in this area so that we, believers in the Lord Jesus Christ can live free in the freedom and liberty that Christ bought for us from curses, sicknesses, diseases, untimely death and eternal death.

If you will take time to read over the scriptures that are discussed in this book and meditate on them, light will come and when light comes, we will no longer walk in darkness or fall for the lies and deceit of the devil in the area of generational curses.

The question to be asked is whether we have been redeemed or not. The answer to that question can not be conditional. It must be a *yes*/*no* answer. If the answer is yes, as we will show through the pages of this book, then any doctrine or belief, however dear they may be to us, if contrary to God's word, must be done away with.

God's word is the only authority in the Body of Christ. The Holy Ghost has also been given to us to guide us into the truth of God's word just as Jesus said, He will glorify the word of God. All supernatural manifestations, doctrines and beliefs must be in line with God's word otherwise, they are null and void. If they are null and void in light of God's word, then we believers must challenge and deprive such doctrines of their power to entangle us again with the yoke of bondage[1] or to run roughshod over us.

The effect of believing the doctrine of the generational curse is that it excuses the devil's works in believers' lives rather than exposing them. When the devil's works are exposed in believers' lives, believers will be able to exercise their authority and destroy them through the name of Jesus. Believers also need to know how to deal with anything in their lives that looks like symptoms of the so-called generational curses or any other curses.

We know from the book of Deuteronomy that curses come in subcategories that include: spiritual death, sickness and diseases, poverty and lack, and untimely death. Any curse you can think of

---

[1] Galatians 5:1

will fall under one or more of these groupings. The ultimate of all curses is untimely death but thanks be to God, we have victory over all curses!

# CHAPTER 1

## Generational Curses and the Old Testament

The first time we read about curses in the Bible was in the Garden of Eden after the fall of man. The devil, in the form of a serpent, approached Eve and tricked her into going against the Word of God saying:

> *[4] ... ye shall not surely die: [5]for God doth know that in the day ye eat thereof, then your eyes shall be opened, and ye shall be as gods, knowing good and evil. (Gen 3:4-5 KJV)*

To cut the long story short, Eve disobeyed God by eating the fruit of the tree that God forbade them from eating and she gave the same fruits to her husband, Adam, and he did eat. Immediately, the glory of God departed from them. They realized they were naked and tried to cover themselves. Shame set in. The curse began even before it was pronounced. They became sorely afraid when they heard the voice of God, even though they had heard God's voice countless times before. Sin changed everything - it gave birth to the curse in their lives and the more the curse grew, the worse they and their lives became.

You will notice that even though Adam and Eve died spiritually immediately, natural death did not take Adam until he was 930 years of age. Another thing to understand is that there is a difference between spiritual death and natural death. In simple terms, spiritual death means separation from God, separation from the life of God - living and walking in darkness. In other words, being ruled over and dominated by Satan. When someone who is separated from God eventually dies, he or she will go to hell. Only the people with the life of God in them can go to heaven after they die.

God, the true judge of the universe had no choice but to pronounce a curse on the serpent, Adam and Eve (Gen 3:14-19). While laying curses as He should, God made way for man's redemption by saying to the serpent (the devil):

> *And I will put enmity between thee and the woman, and between thy seed and her seed; it shall bruise thy head, and thou shalt bruise his heel. (Gen 3:15 KJV).*

The seed of the woman shall bruise the head of the serpent and that was what happened when Jesus died on the Cross. He went to the grave to defeat the devil and rose victorious from the dead as the King of Kings and Lord of Lords with the ability to give eternal life and dominion over the devil to whosoever will believe and trust in His Holy name.

From the first instance of the curse being mentioned in the Bible, we see a close relationship between curses and sin. Without sin, there was no curse and vice versa. It follows, therefore, that removing sin will rid a person of curses. That is what Jesus did for the believers in Christ.

Now, there is the popular belief about sin and by implication curses passing from one generation to another. While that may be true under the Old Testament, such punishment is not recorded in the New Testament because the grace of our Lord Jesus is mightier than any curse, and the blood shed by the Lord at Calvary far surpasses in power and glory any sin the devil can invent.

After the children of Israel were brought out of Egypt by God's mighty hand, in Exodus chapter 20, God warned them through Moses to stay away from idols and not to have any other gods beside him.

*⁴ Thou shalt not make unto thee any graven image or any likeness of anything that is in heaven above, or that is in the earth beneath, or that is in the water under the earth: ⁵ thou shalt not bow down thyself to them, nor serve them: for I the Lord thy God am a jealous God, visiting the iniquity of the fathers upon the children unto the third and fourth generation of them that hate me; ⁶ and shewing mercy unto thousands of them that love me, and keep my commandments.* (Exodus 20:4-6 KJV)

God loved the children of Israel so much that he pre-warned them against doing things that would bring curses into their lives. If they disobeyed and curses came upon them, it would be correct to say that the children of Israel brought curses upon themselves rather than God bringing curses on them. In verse 5, God describes Himself as a jealous God who can visit the iniquity of the fathers upon the children unto the third and fourth generation of them that hate Him. The key phrase in that pronouncement is "upon them that hate me". Anyone who hates God will have a curse on them automatically. The same was said by Jesus that "he who does not believe is judged already." That is a curse.

In the same breath, God said He shows mercy unto thousands of those who love Him and keep His commandment. Now, this is the perfect will of God. From the creation of man, God has been working overtime to get man to do His will so He can continue to show His mercy because He is a good and merciful God. This is why the children of Israel learnt to say, "The Lord is good, and His mercy endures forever". Praise God!

## The Curse Upon David's House

After David, the King of Israel committed adultery by sleeping with Bathsheba, the wife of Uriah the Hittite and orchestrated the death of Uriah, God sent Prophet Nathan to confront David with his sin and to pass judgment on David for that sin. 2 Samuel 12:7-12:

> *⁷ And Nathan said to David, Thou art the man. Thus, saith the Lord God of Israel, I anointed thee king over Israel, and I delivered thee out of the hand of Saul; ⁸ And I gave thee thy master's house, and thy master's wives into thy bosom, and gave thee the house of Israel and Judah; and if that had been too little, I would moreover have given unto thee such and such things. ⁹ Wherefore hast thou despised the commandment of the Lord, to do evil in his sight? thou hast killed Uriah the Hittite with the sword, and hast taken his wife to be thy wife, and hast slain him*

*with the sword of the children of Ammon. <sup>10</sup> Now therefore*

*with the sword of the children of Ammon. ¹⁰ Now therefore the sword shall never depart from thine house; because thou hast despised me, and hast taken the wife of Uriah the Hittite to be thy wife. ¹¹ Thus, saith the Lord, Behold, I will raise up evil against thee out of thine own house, and I will take thy wives before thine eyes, and give them unto thy neighbour, and he shall lie with thy wives in the sight of this sun. ¹² For thou didst it secretly: but I will do this thing before all Israel, and before the sun. (2 Samuel 12:7-12 KJV)*

A curse came upon David and his house because of his wickedness in sinning against the living God. We see from reading the story of David that a lot of evil happened in his household. One son raped his sister, and another son killed the one who had raped her. His son Absalom made himself king and fought his father with the determination to kill him. Another son after that also declared himself king and on and on his troubles went.

Notwithstanding the curse, God blessed David's son Solomon, who later became a king in his place. As long as Solomon served and obeyed the Lord, the curse stayed away from him. We also see that at the end of Solomon's life when he became old, he got carried away by his foreign wives and fell into idol worship, for which God also judged him. After the reign of Solomon, the kingdom split into two – Israel and Judah. The two kingdoms had successive kings, such as Ahab and Manasseh, who did badly, while others like Jehoshaphat and Josiah walked in the way of the Lord.

The point is that even where there is a curse that can travel from one generation to another, the behaviour of one generation determines whether the curse will pass on to them or not. King David's descendants, like Jehoshaphat and Josiah, enjoyed the blessings of the Lord, while others like Ahab died like dogs and suffered defeat most of their lives. It suffices therefore that even under the Old Testament, one can stop a curse upon his life by serving God and taking heed to His commandments.

## "Generational Curses" - What are they? Are they real?

Again, since the term "generational curse" is not mentioned in the Bible, it is difficult to say exactly what it is. Whatever definition is ascribed to the term will be subjective at best. Even if generational curses are real as far as people's experiences go, they are not real or capable of being real in the life of a child of God – someone who has been born again – the redeemed of the Lord.

The Bible teaches that the devil is the god of this world, who blinds the minds of those who believe not.[2] Notice the scripture says, "them which believe not" not "us who have been born again and believe". Satan's influence and dominion are binding on unbelievers but broken over the believers. We are no more under his influence; we have been redeemed. Consequently, even if generational curses are real, they are not capable of being real in the life of a believer.

Those in the body of Christ who believe that generational curses are real and should be broken off a believer's neck, define the concept as negative, curse-like symptoms that are handed down through natural lineages and seem to run from one generation to another. The proponents of this so-called doctrine of generational curses don't seem to believe that the shed blood of Jesus is strong enough to release a born-again believer from curses.

An example of what they call generational curses is this: a grandfather experienced an evil or catastrophic event such as a heart attack or a kind of sickness at age fifty. His son had a similar experience, either at the same age or close. The grandchild is also now experiencing the same illness around the same age as the

---

[2] 2 Corinthians 4:4

grandfather and the father. This is now interpreted to mean that there is a generational curse affecting the family.

The reasoning behind this concept becomes flawed and defective when we apply the concept to someone who has been born again, on whom no curse can align due to the work that Christ did in him or her at redemption. It is disheartening and pathetic to see that some believers in the Lord Jesus, for whom the precious blood of Jesus was shed, could believe that generational curses, or any curse for that matter, could affect them.

Now, you need to know that whatever you believe and embrace, however wrong, will eventually become your experience. This holds whether what you are believing is in line with the word of God or not. I also would like to state, unreservedly and unequivocally, that the devil doesn't have the power to put a curse on a child of God. However, if you, a child of God, choose to operate away from your covenant in Christ and let him run roughshod over you, even though you have authority over him and his works, whatever you suffer will not be God's fault but yours.

We need to start renewing our minds so we can think and believe in line with God's word. When we do, we will be quick to identify the devil's schemes, so you as a believer in Christ can exercise your authority to quash his works and walk in the abundant life that Jesus came to give to us.

# CHAPTER 2

## The Old and the New Covenants

To enjoy the blessings of God in Christ, a believer must gain, maintain and grow in a good understanding of the difference between the Old and the New Covenants. There is indeed a difference between the two. A lot changed under the new covenant, and failure to appreciate this fact will cause a believer in Christ Jesus to live below their privileges in life. The new covenant is also the covenant under which every believer in Christ Jesus lives.

Am I saying we should not care much about the Old Covenant as revealed in what we call the Old Testament? Absolutely not! In writing to New Covenant believers at Corinth about the importance of a believer having a good grasp of the Old Testament text of the Bible, Apostle Paul in 1 Corinthians 10:1-11 writes:

> *¹ Moreover, brethren, I do not want you to be unaware that all our fathers were under the cloud, all passed through the sea, ² all were baptized into Moses in the cloud and in the sea, ³ all ate the same spiritual food, ⁴ and all drank the same spiritual drink. For they drank of that*

*spiritual Rock that followed them, and that Rock was Christ. ⁵ But with most of them God was not well pleased, for their bodies were scattered in the wilderness. ⁶ Now these things became our examples, to the intent that we should not lust after evil things as they also lusted. ⁷ And do not become idolaters as were some of them. As it is written, "The people sat down to eat and drink, and rose up to play". ⁸ Nor let us commit sexual immorality, as some of them did, and in one day twenty-three thousand fell; ⁹ nor let us tempt Christ, as some of them also tempted, and were destroyed by serpents; ¹⁰ nor complain, as some of them also complained, and were destroyed by the destroyer. ¹¹ Now all these things happened to them as examples, and they were written for our admonition, upon whom the ends of the ages have come. (1 Corinthians 10:1-11 NKJV)*

Read over verse 11 again. It says that the things Paul wrote about from verses 1 to 10 of the chapter happened to them as examples and were written for our admonition. He is saying that the Old Testament texts are written for us to have a point of reference. That means that we should emulate what the Old Testament saints did that was right and avoid what they did that was wrong.

You see, God has not changed. He is the same God He has always been and will forever be. What displeases Him then, displeases Him now and what pleased Him then, pleases Him now.

Another reason why we must read and understand the Old Testament is that, like the new, it is the Word of God that lives and abides forever. Nevertheless, we should spend more time understanding what Christ did for us under the New Covenant. For example, as a New Covenant believer, you don't attain righteousness by your good works. You were created as a new creation and the righteousness of God in Christ (2 Corinthians 5:17 & 21).

Another unique spiritual truth we must understand is that of the name of Jesus, by which a believer in Christ can demonstrate his or her authority over the devil, demonic activities, sickness, diseases and any such things. According to Ephesians chapter 2, the New Covenant believer's authority reaches the heavens, the earth and beneath the earth. It is an incomparable authority. To buttress this point, let's consider two passages of scriptures – one from the Old Testament and the second from the New Testament.

*And I will rebuke the devourer for your sakes, so that he will not destroy the fruit of your ground, Nor shall the vine fail to bear fruit for you in the field," Says the Lord of hosts; (Malachi 3:11 NKJV)*

God promised the children of Israel that if they would honour Him with their tithes and offerings, as He commanded them; He would rebuke the devourer for them. From the study of the Word, we know who the devourer is. It is the devil whom Jesus describes in John 10:10 as a thief who comes to steal, kill and destroy.

James 4:7 says *"7 Therefore submit to God. Resist the devil and he will flee from you"*. Concerning New Covenant believers, the Lord Jesus said:

*17 And these signs will follow those who believe: In My name, they will cast out demons; they will speak with new tongues; 18 they will take up serpents; and if they drink anything deadly, it will by no means hurt them; they will lay hands on the sick, and they will recover. (Mark 16:17-18 NKJV).*

This same truth repeatedly resounds throughout the New Testament.

The core of the New Covenant is the removal of the sinful nature by the shed blood of Jesus, which in turn makes a believer in Christ a child of God, having the same Holy Spirit, power, ability and enablement as the Lord Jesus Himself. When believers get hold of this truth, they stop to see themselves as beggars who are always seeking and trying to gain God's approval. For example, for many years in my ministry, I have tried my best to teach believers how to pray for the sick. I know we loosely call it "praying for the sick" however, nowhere in the New Testament do we see the Lord Jesus or the Apostles pray for the sick. What they did was more like commanding sicknesses and diseases to leave and disappear and they did.

The healing of the man at the Gate called Beautiful in Acts chapter 3 by Peter and John is the prime example of this point. They commanded the man in the name of Jesus to rise and walk, and he did. Apostle Paul in Acts 14 did the same with the man impotent in his feet who never walked. Paul said to the man with a loud voice "Stand upright on your feet" and the man was healed. Apostle Peter used the same command of faith with Aeneas in Acts chapter 9, a man who had been bedfast for 8 years and was paralyzed. Peter said to him *"Aeneas, Jesus the Christ heals you. Arise and make your bed*". Glory to God! The man arose immediately and was completely healed.

The point I am trying to make is that it is a good understanding of the New Testament that will give you this kind of knowledge, and when the knowledge becomes a revelation knowledge to you, you will be able to do what Peter, John and Paul did in the passages we discussed. The Lord Jesus in the book of John chapter 14 verse 12 says "The work I do they (that believe) shall do also and greater works than this shall they do because I go to my father".

Notwithstanding your knowledge and understanding, if you have been born again and filled with the Holy Spirit, you have this same power that Peter, John, Paul and the rest of the apostles had and operated by. However, it takes knowledge, understanding and your action of faith to release the power that resides in you. When you learn to release this power, no symptoms of generational curses will be able to hang around you. You will be a no-go area for Satan because he knows that if he comes around you, he will be resisted and defeated.

Now, you can see that going through life believing a generational curse is over your life will make you powerless and defeated. What you have in you is the power of the Holy Spirit which is more powerful than any curse or anything the enemy can come up with. This is an area where believers must know the truth for themselves. When you have this knowledge and you get to a place or situation where the enemy's activities are suspected, you can declare to the enemy through Christ who is in you and command his work to be suspended until you leave the place or the situation.

It follows, therefore, that a believer who will walk in his or her New Covenant privileges cannot go about listening to people who tell you there is a demon in you. Or people who tell you, there is a curse over your life. I don't care how famous they are; anyone who tells you that you have something the New Testament says you don't have, or who talks you out of what the New Testament says belongs to you, is not your friend, and you should be careful about listening to them. The Bible is our final authority. We have what it says we have and can do what it says we can do. The reverse is also true: we don't have what it says we cannot have, and we cannot be limited by what it says we are not limited by.

A New Covenant believer has the Holy Spirit living in him not demons of evil spirits. 1 John 4:4 says

*⁴ You are of God, little children, and have overcome them because He who is in you is greater than he who is in the world. (1 John 4:4 NKJV)*

Who is in the world? Satan, the devil and evil spirits, demons, sicknesses, diseases and the like. God is saying that the Holy Spirit in you is greater than whatever is in the world. He is greater than the god of this world system, the devil. 1 John 2:14b says:

*I have written to you, young men, because you are strong, and the Word of God abides in you, and you have overcome the wicked one. (1 John 2:14b NKJV)*

My friends, I don't know how you can believe these scriptures and maintain a mindset of faith and victory while accepting that a curse may be upon your life. The teaching that believers can operate under generational curses is unscriptural. Nonetheless, a believer can, through a lack of knowledge and refusal to exercise the authority they have in the name of Jesus, be bound by the symptoms of curses. Satan will oppress a believer if he/she allows him, but thank God, we don't have to. Satan has no authority over us. Jesus gave us authority over him.

Brother Hagin, of blessed memory, said that the New Covenant includes the blessings of the Old plus more. The Bible calls it a better covenant based on better promises. A lot has been provided for us in the New Covenant because of the eternal sacrifice of our Lord Jesus. Our Father God wants us to live in the consciousness of our rights and privileges in Christ.

Let me give an analogy to drive the point home. Let's say someone is a Canadian citizen. Their citizenship comes with certain rights and privileges. At the minimum, this person is entitled to the rights and privileges of the Charter of Rights and Freedoms of Canada. The rights and privileges of a newly born Canadian citizen or a newly naturalized Canadian citizen are the same as those of the Prime Minister of Canada, where private citizenship rights are concerned. The level to which a private citizen and the prime minister exercise their private rights depends on their understanding and enforcement of the rights. This is true for God's children. What you don't know, you will not enforce and without enforcement, there is no enjoyment.

Sadly, many believers in Christ today see themselves as being under the Old Covenant due to their lack of knowledge. Born-again believers are not, and can no longer be, subject to any curse, generational or otherwise, because of what Jesus did for them. It doesn't matter whether their earthly father, like King David, brought a curse upon himself due to his sin. You, as a member of the family of God, cannot be under a curse. The devil does not have the power to impose himself on a believer in Christ through sin, curses, sickness or diseases unless they let him.

# CHAPTER 3

# A Doctrine Rooted in Experience

If you spend any length of time listening or discussing the concept of generational curses with its proponents, even though they will not be able to give you a chapter and verse in the New Testament, they will have a litany of experiences to prove the reality of the concept.

Experiences are a shaky ground upon which a spiritual belief should be based. In the mouth of two or three witnesses shall every word be established[3] not through experiences. The witness we are referring to here is the witness of the word of God[4], the Bible. People sometimes make the mistake of thinking that whatever they experience must be the truth. We need to re-educate ourselves to realize that experiences come through our senses which means they may be deceptive. We need to always go with what God says in His word.

By exalting our experiences or that of others above God's Word, the Bible, we will get ourselves in trouble spiritually. I have paid close attention to preachers who go about convincing Christians

---

[3] 2 Corinthians 13:1
[4] 1 John 5:7

that generational curses are working in their lives that need to be broken. In all the times I have listened to them, I can not recall a time, not once, that any of them was able to justify their doctrine through any scriptures. Whenever they attempt to do so, their Bible explanations to justify the doctrine are vague and confusing at best.

Something however interesting about the proponents of generational curses is that, they usually have convincing stories either of their own or that of other so-called "strong" Christians that justify the reality and the hold of generational curses over a believer. Any experience, no matter how spiritual, angelic, spectacular or otherwise that is not based on the Bible and for which you can not come up with a chapter and verse, particularly in the New Testament, is not and can not be of God!

We also know that the cultural influences; unbiblical experiences and insinuations which some Christians experienced before they got born again are sometimes carried over into their Christian life. What we need to do is what Paul admonishes us when he says we should put on the new man which is in the likeness of God and created in righteousness and true holiness[5]. We need to get a good

---

[5] Ephesians 4:24

grasp on the spiritual truth to know that when someone gets born again; in the realm of the spirit, he or she is neither an African born again, a Chinese born again, an Indian born again nor an American born again. You are simply a new creation in Christ to whom old things are passed away and all things have become new[6].

Experiences, good or bad, should not run the life of a new creation in Christ. A new creation in Christ must allow God's word to affect, influence and run his or her life so that God's word can create new holy experiences in their lives that will be consistent with their new nature.

An experience that proclaims the inferiority of the recreated human spirit and exalts the ability of Satan over a believer is not an experience to be embraced or celebrated. They are to be rejected and taken authority over in Jesus' name. On his or her weakest day, a believer in Christ Jesus is much more powerful than the devil because greater is He that is in him or her than he (the devil) that is in the world[7].

---

[6] 2 Corinthians 5:17
[7] 1 John 4:4

Someone once told me a story of how a witch doctor had put a spell on a believer which caused him to become deaf and it took several days of fasting without any food or water to deliver the Christian. See, stories like this sound very religious and spiritual especially if told by a minister or a friend you consider a mature Christian. Brothers and sisters, we should never hold any man or woman, no matter how wonderfully they are used by God, to where we esteem them higher than the word of God. Paul said, "Be ye, followers of me, even as I also am of Christ[8]". What that means is that our esteem for Paul should only be to the level of his submission to the word of God and Christ. The moment he stops following Christ, we are no longer supposed to follow him or his doctrines or teachings that are not consistent with the Bible. The great Apostle Paul himself buttressed this when he said:

> *But though we, or an angel from heaven, preach any other gospel unto you than that, which we have preached unto you, let him be accursed (Galatians 1:8 NKJV).*

---

[8] 1 Corinthians 11:1

The same will hold for any man or woman of God in our lives. The Body of Christ only has one infallible head, Lord and Master and his name is Jesus who also is the Word of God.

If we re-examine the story about the witch doctor casting a spell on a believer, its inconsistency with the teaching of the Bible will be clearly obvious. Is it not interesting to note that there is not one place in the New Testament where the Bible records a spell being cast on either a child of God or a devil being cast out of a believer? I know this may sound shocking to some Christians. Rather than getting mad at the statement and throwing the book away, what you need to do is a Bible search on the subject and if you see such an account, then don't accept what you just read. On the other hand, if your search reveals and confirms what I said to be true then it is time we changed our erroneous beliefs that have the potentials to rob us of our authority in Christ.

Under the Old Covenant, God made it clear that no one can curse the people whom He has blessed. A spell by definition is an evil charm or incantation meant to carry a curse. Conversely, when God says no one can curse the people that are blessed by Him that will also mean that no one can cast a spell on the people that are blessed by God. A New Testament believer is a no-curse, no-spell, Holy Ghost-free zone that the devil dares not and cannot violate. The problem is that through our ignorance of God's word, we let the devil deceive us into undermining the unsurpassed authority we have been given in Christ.

If God's people under the Old Covenant could have it so good that God declared that no one could curse or put a spell on them because they have been blessed by Him, how much more us who are under the new covenant that is based upon better promises!

Oh! how we need to educate ourselves today in God's word by studying to show ourselves approved to God, a workman that needs not to be ashamed, rightly dividing the word of truth[9]. If we understand and live our lives by the simple concept that if it is not in the Bible, it cannot be true; we will never fall prey to any unbiblical doctrine or concept like the one being addressed in this book.

Another thought that is worthy of meditation is this. There is not one record of the early Christians going on several days of fasting and prayers before casting out devils or healing the sick. No, not after they received power and the Holy Ghost came upon them in Acts chapter 2. Now, I don't want you to misunderstand me to think that I am suggesting that fasting or praying is wrong.

---

[9] 1 Timothy 2:15

What I am saying is that we have so much authority in Christ and in Jesus' name that we can do the works of Christ as quickly as they show up. The devil is not more powerful than Jesus neither is he more powerful than you if you have been born again. On the contrary, you have enormous power over him and his cohorts such that when you resist him, he flees from you (as in terror)[10].

I have heard ministers say things like, "Well, if Reverend ABC could be taken by cancer and die, it can happen to anyone". Now, that is elevating others' experiences above the Word of God. Why, if I may ask, would you want to destroy yourself through the words of your mouth just because of Reverend ABC's experience? Reverend ABC's experience, as sad as that may be to a good reverend, does not negate God's word. God's word is as powerful as it will always be before, during and after Reverend ABC's experience. We don't discount Reverend ABC's experience nor judge him. We rejoice with them that do rejoice, and weep (or sorrow) with them that weep (or sorrow)[11]. Even at that, we keep trusting and believing in what the word says.

---

[10] James 5:7
[11] Romans 12:15

We should be like Mary the mother of Jesus whose response to God's word was "...be it unto me according to thy word".[12]

Friends, let us put our trust in Reverend Jesus and our faith in His Word that says, by his stripes I was healed and that says: no weapon that is formed or fashioned against me (including cancers, sicknesses, diseases, poverty, curses and untimely death) shall prosper. That is what we should say and we will see God fulfil the numbers of our days according to His promises in His word.

Another thing that has become a stronghold in the minds of some Christians is justifying the devil's works in their lives based on the part of the world they reside. How ignorant can this be? There is no distance in the realm of the spirit nor is God limited based on a country's postal or zip code or a lack of one. He is God Almighty who works miracles through His people when they are bold to act upon His Word irrespective of where they live. The devil is the same devil and demons are demons notwithstanding where they may be found. Just the same way that Jesus dealt with them in Jerusalem and the surrounding towns and villages in those days and the early Christians dealt with them everywhere they went, is the same way we can deal with them today wherever

---

[12] Luke 1:38

we live. We have authority over them. Jesus gave that authority to us and they will obey us when we speak to them in faith and boldness in the name of Jesus. We believers have authority over Satan and his cohorts in Asia, Africa, North America, Europe, South America, Australia and everywhere they or their works may be found upon God's green earth.

The Bible says

> [9] *Wherefore God also hath highly exalted him and given him a name which is above every name:* [10] *that at the name of Jesus every knee should bow, of things in heaven, and things in earth, and things under the earth;* [11] *and that every tongue should confess that Jesus Christ is Lord, to the glory of God the Father (Philippians 2:9-11 KJV).*

Notice, that the Bible does not limit the authority of the name of Jesus to the earth but extends it to the heavens and beneath the earth. If you ponder on that for a moment, you will realize that the devil cannot escape the name of Jesus in your mouth because of your geographical location. Stop agreeing with his lies!

# CHAPTER 4

## Understanding the Nature of Man

Man is a spirit; he has a soul and lives in a body. The "you" that I see outside when I meet you and shake hands with you is not your real self. Your real man is the man on the inside, which the Bible calls the inner man or the hidden man of the heart. 1Thessalonians 5:23 says

> *Now may the God of peace Himself sanctify you completely; and may your whole spirit, soul, and body be preserved blameless at the coming of our Lord Jesus Christ.*
> (1 Thessalonians 5:23 NKJV)

This scripture makes it clear that you are not just the body we see when we look at you. You're more than the hands we shake or the face we recognise. You are much more than that. Man is a spirit; he has a soul and lives in a physical body. This knowledge is very important to a successful Christian living on this earth. The Lord Jesus and most of the writers of the New Testament preached this important truth. In Matthew 10:28, our Lord Jesus said:

*And fear not them which kill the body but are not able to
kill the soul: but rather fear him which is able to destroy
both soul and body in hell. (Matthew10:28 KJV)*

This means we are not just the body that people see when they look at us. Making this same point, Apostle Paul says:

*For we know that if our earthly house of this tabernacle
were dissolved, we have a building of God, a house not
made with hands, eternal in the heavens. (2 Cor 5:1 KJV)*

Here, Apostle Paul likens our body to an earthly house, a tabernacle. Thinking that you are just the body we see is akin to thinking that the house you live in is the real you. Just as you leave your house to go to work, when you die, your real self will depart to be with Christ if you have been born again, and your body, which is the house you lived in while on earth will be left here somewhere in the grave. Thanks be to God, our bodies will be changed someday when our Lord splits the sky and descends with a shout, according to the Word of the Lord.

Notice what Apostle Peter said in 2 Peter 1:12-15 about his death

*¹²For this reason I will not be negligent to remind you always of these things, though you know and are established in the present truth. ¹³Yes, I think it is right, as long as I am in this tent, to stir you up by reminding you, ¹⁴knowing that shortly I must put off my tent, just as our Lord Jesus Christ showed me. ¹⁵Moreover I will be careful to ensure that you always have a reminder of these things after my decease. (2 Peter 1:12-15 NKJV)*

As Paul likened his body to a tabernacle, Peter described his body as a tent – a temporary dwelling. He says he will put off this tent, which means after his death, he will continue to live in heaven with Christ without his tent, his body.

To clarify, a man or woman is a spirit who has a soul and lives in a physical body. The spirit is the part that is born again and where the Holy Spirit lives hence, we are the temple of the Holy Spirit. The soul is the seat of our emotion, will, intellect – our mind. As mentioned, our body is the house we live in. I like how Brother Hagin explains it. He said with our spirit, we contact God and the spirit realm; with our mind, we contact the intellectual world, and with our body, we contact the world around us. It is with our body that we feel, touch, taste and smell. A believer who doesn't know the difference between the tripartite nature of man will live a life ruled by his flesh. This is what the Bible describes as being carnal – flesh ruled – flesh controlled, responding only to the dictates of the flesh.

The dealings of God are with the man's spirit. Jesus was referring to the spirit of man, the real man on the inside when he said man shall not live by bread alone but by every Word that proceeds out of the mouth of God. It is a disadvantage when a believer can't see beyond the natural. It takes faith to see beyond the natural to believe the Word of God and act upon the Word of God. A believer must accept the Word of God as the truth and as the final authority, such that they can stake their lives on whatever it says. According to Romans 10:10:

> For with the heart one believes unto righteousness, and
> with the mouth confession is made unto salvation.
> (Romans 10:10 NKJV)

The heart is the same as the spirit hence, the verse means with the spirit man one believes. You can't believe with your mind or with your body. This is the reason God gave the command to Joshua not to let the word of God depart from his mouth and to meditate in it day and night. Why meditate? So, the Word can drop in his spirit, be mixed with faith, and become a reality in his life.

According to God, the outcome of the instruction for Joshua will be prosperity and good success.

It follows that if the Bible says,

> *Surely there is no enchantment against Jacob, Neither is there any divination against Israel: According to this time it shall be said of Jacob and of Israel, what hath God wrought! (Numbers 23:23 KJV)*

Then, the believer must believe it and mix their faith with the Word, notwithstanding what the enemy may be whispering to their ears. Look at what God says in Colossians 1:

> [12] *Giving thanks unto the Father, which hath made us meet to be partakers of the inheritance of the saints in light:* [13] *Who hath delivered us from the power of darkness, and hath translated us into the kingdom of his dear Son:* [14] *In whom we have redemption through his blood, even the forgiveness of sins. (Colossians 1: 12-14 NKJV)*

There are some profound provisions for the believers in this passage which you, as a believer must accept as the truth, mix faith with it in your heart, and put the Word of God in your mouth until it becomes a reality in your life. Verse 12 says that, God has made us meet or qualified to be partakers of His inheritance. This is not something that happens when we get to heaven but something that has already happened. Verse 13 emphasizes that God has already delivered you from the power of darkness including generational curses, and all other curses.

Finally, the passage says that, as born-again believers, we have obtained redemption through the blood of Jesus and the forgiveness of sins. This is a reality in heaven, but through our faith, you and I can make it a reality here on earth. We mix our faith with what God has said while holding our fears and natural circumstances as inconsequential in the light of the Word of the living God, who cannot lie.

## God and His Man Adam

The true story according to the Bible was that God created Adam in His image[13] and pronounced a blessing[14] on Him which is to be fruitful, multiply, replenish the earth, and have dominion over it and things on the earth in all forms and nature.

---

[13] Genesis 1:26-31

[14] Blessing is a supernatural empowerment to prosper. In other words, to be fruitful, replenish, multiply and to have dominion (Kenneth Copeland)

God also planted a garden called the Garden of Eden[15] where he placed His man, Adam and his wife. In the garden, God abundantly supplied Adam and Eve with everything they needed. Adam was a supernatural man living by the pronounced blessing of God. The blessing was upon him and working in his life. This fact can be corroborated by the awesome manner in which he named all the animals and wild beasts that walked upon the surface of the earth as God created them.

Adam had such soundness of mind that he did not duplicate names for the animals even though there was no record of him keeping a journal of the previously used names. He did not forget to name any animal whatsoever. He enjoyed such dominion over the animals, wild, venomous or otherwise that we had no record of him getting bitten or attacked by any of them even though he must have gone really close to tigers, leopards, poisonous snakes and other dangerous animals. Adam also had wealth items like gold, bdellium and onyx stone[16] among others in the garden.

With all the blessings of God upon and in Adam's life, the only restriction he had was not to eat of a particular tree called the "tree of the knowledge of good and evil". God almighty by His

---

[15] Genesis 2:7-9
[16] See 3.

command, told Adam that he would die the day he ate of the tree. Adam continued in the blessing until the serpent (the devil) came and tricked his wife Eve, and Adam went along, disobeying God by eating from the tree contrary to God's commandments to him. Adam subsequently died spiritually as God said they would. His spiritual death set in motion natural death, sicknesses, diseases, poverty and lack as well as all manner of curses.

The Bible records that the glory of God which covered Mr. & Mrs. Adam by the reason of the blessing departed from them. For the very first time ever since this God's man was created, a man who was not afraid of anything that creeps, who was in close fellowship with the Almighty God and talked to God as he pleased; stated that when he heard the voice of God, he was afraid and had to hide from the voice of God[17].

Notice that for the very first time in his existence, Adam said "I was afraid". This is the evidence that the devil who is the owner of the spirit of fear and torment had come in to take over. Fear is the evidence of the departure of God's glory, the absence or evaporation of the blessing, the inception of sin and the birth of the sin nature. Knowing the lies of the devil and torments that

---

[17] Genesis 3: 10

accompany fear, God said to the New Testament believers "God has not given us the spirit of fear but of power and of love and of a sound mind[18]".

In addition to what we discussed above about the blessing, the following are some other important things to note. First, God is the only one who can bless. Second, God only had to pronounce the blessing on Adam once and it stuck to him – His pronouncement was needed only once for his entire life. Third, the blessing is transferrable. Whosoever or whatsoever Adam, the blessed and blessing empowered man blessed was blessed with God's blessing as if it was God that directly pronounced the blessing on such person or thing. We also see this same principle in the life of Abraham. Whosoever blessed Abraham was automatically blessed by God[19] and whosoever Abraham blessed was blessed.

Finally, because of Adam's disobedience and in line with God's original pronouncements, God was forced to pronounce a curse on the serpent (Satan), Adam and the woman. The sinful nature came into God's man and because he was the representative of mankind, Adam's death reigned on all men and women after him.

---

[18] 2 Timothy 1:7
[19] Genesis 12:13

# Death Reigned Until Redemption

Death reigned upon mankind through the curse that Adam's disobedience attracted. The Bible teaches that "...death reigned from Adam to Moses, even over them that had not sinned after the similitude of Adam's transgression...[20]"

Even though death now reigned and legally so, as severe as the curse and its effects were, God, throughout the Old Testament devised plans and found ways to shield His covenant people, those who obeyed him, from the effect of the curse. God's plans under the Old Covenant were only able to shield His people from the curse but could not remove the curse in its entirety until the second Adam; the Lord Jesus came to redeem mankind. Jesus came and paid in full for the transgressions of Adam and all other humans who ever came after him. He satisfied the demands of justice and the entire mankind became redeemed.

What does it mean to redeem? Redemption is to regain possession of something in exchange for payment. To buy back with a higher price than the price the person or the item got lost by. Through the redemption work of the Lord Jesus, mankind was bought back from the curse and the effects thereof. Whosoever will

---

[20] Romans 5:14

accept and receive Jesus' work on the cross, his burial and resurrection as well as confess Him as Lord today will exchange the sinful nature inherited from Adam for God's righteousness. A new spirit will be created in him which is in the image, likeness, and nature of God.

Therefore, we who have been born again, believers in the Lord Jesus have been redeemed from the quilt of sin which includes all curses and any effects associated with them. We are now the carriers of God's blessing. The blessing has the power not only to neutralize curses but to blot them out completely. Jesus knew this to be true when he said,

> *Verily I say unto you, whatsoever ye shall bind on earth shall be bound in heaven: and whatsoever ye shall loose on earth shall be loosed in heaven (Matthew 18:18 KJV).*

He also said,

> *[21]...as my Father hath sent me, even so, send I you. [22]And when he had said this, he breathed on them, and saith unto them, receive ye the Holy Ghost: [23]Whosoever sins ye remit, they are remitted unto them; and whosoever sins ye retain, they are retained. (John 20: 21b-23)*

Every single person under the New Testament has been blessed with this same blessing. The blessing has an untold and unquantifiable power to neutralize curses - generational or not. A pronouncement of the blessing will cause curses to seize with the power of the word of God reversing the effects of curses, undoing whatever the devil had done.

We should be smart enough to know that not everybody will accept the blessing that is provided in Christ. This is why, we Christians have been commanded to preach the Good News to all people to let them know that they do not need to continue living under the curse anymore as they have been blessed by God in Christ with a way of escape widely made available to all. All that needs to be done is to confess the Lord Jesus with your mouth and believe in your heart that God has raised him from the dead[21] and you shall be saved. Along with instant salvation, comes the automatic breaking and blotting out of all curses.

If we follow the biblical reasoning above, it will be clear to us that a doctrine that calls for the breaking of generational curses, or any other curses for that matter of a believer, is erroneous and foreign to the teachings of the word of God. See, we have this issue in

---

[21] Romans 9:10-11

the Body of Christ where people encourage us to ask for what we already have or to pray to become who Christ already made us. Whenever we beg God to make us what we already are or ask Him to give us what we already possess in Christ, what we are saying to Jesus in essence is that we don't believe that He actually did what He said He did in His word. By so doing, we step outside of faith into unbelief and unbelief can not please God; only faith does.

Faith is believing and acting on God's word. Faith agrees with God and thanks Him for whatever He says He has done for us in His word. We walk by faith, not by sight[22] or by our natural experiences. We need to learn to reject and say no to preaching and teachings that draw us back to unbelief and doubt. We are faithful children of God just as our father is a faithful God. Let us agree with what He says and thank Him for it and we will see the manifestation of His truth in our lives.

God has reconciled Himself to mankind. What is left to be done is for men and women to reconcile themselves to God by accepting God's solution and mediator; the man Christ Jesus. When they do, they will become a new creation in Christ for

---

[22] 2 Corinthians 5:7

whom old things are passed away and all things have become new[23]. To a new creature, curses and afflictions are things of old, they are things of the past, and they have been done away with. No deliverance from them is needed because they do not exist. How do you deliver yourself of what you don't have or something you are not capable of having?

Before we proceed from our discussion about redemption, I would like to revisit our definition of what it means to be redeemed. We said it is "to regain possession of something in exchange for payment". It is only logical to reason that you are willing to make this payment to regain something that is of greater value, more valuable and of superior quality/quantity to the cost of what was lost. The great Apostle Peter made this clear to us when he said, "…ye were not redeemed with corruptible things as silver and gold… but with the precious blood of Christ, as of a lamb without blemish and spot…[24]". Silver and gold were not enough; it took the precious blood of Christ to buy us back and regain the lost blessing for us.

The good news, ladies and gentlemen, is that what we gained through the sacrifice of the Lord (Adam II) far exceeded what we

---

[23] 2 Corinthians 5:17
[24] 1 Peter 1: 18-19

lost in the garden through the disobedience of Adam I. The blessing and the status that came through Christ are neither neutralizable nor violable. They are as superior as the price that was paid for them. They are also as divine as the one who gave Himself for us as sacrifice.

King David, functioning as a prophet under the Old Covenant saw into the future and admonished the redeemed of the Lord, the New Testament Christians to proclaim their victory. What should they say, King David? They should say that they have been redeemed and also proclaim same both to God and to whosoever cares to listen that they have indeed been redeemed by the Lord Jesus Christ. This has nothing to do with what they can feel or see but speaking in line with their new status in God through Christ. We now have a new way of talking. I am the redeemed of the Lord and I say so. He has redeemed me from the hands of my enemy. I am no longer under the curse but in the blessing of my father, praise God!

## The New Testament Approach

I would like, at this juncture, to make it clear to you that, the most important thing a believer can do is to renew his or her mind.

Apostle Paul calls it a transformation and a spiritual worship[25]. What is a believer to renew his or her mind to? First and foremost, a believer must renew his or her mind to the word of God as it relates to the differences between the Old and the New Testament dispensations. He or she needs to know there are different rules to live by under the Old as there is a new set of rules under the New.

The New Testament is superior to the Old even though both are God's dispensations. When we talk about the Old Testament being done away with and the New taking its place, some Christians get unnecessarily defensive and agitated. They query whether the Old Testament is not God's word? Questions like this are unnecessary and somewhat ridiculous. Of course, the Old Testament is as much God's word as the New but the fact is that the New Testament is the dispensation of everlasting redemption which God designed for believers to live today.

The Bible states

> *[7]For if that first covenant had been faultless, then should no place have been sought for the second. [8]For finding fault with*

---

[25] Romans 12:1-2 (Amplified version)

*them, he saith, Behold, the days come, saith the Lord, when I will make a new covenant with the house of Israel and with the house of Judah. (Hebrew 8:7-8 KJV)*

It was God Himself who said that the Old Covenant was faulty. If God in His wisdom deemed the new covenant to be the covenant suited enough for believers in Christ, why would any thinking Christian want to remain under the old covenant? The New Testament is based on better promises. Believers today must be New Testament taught rather than being religiously brainwashed[26]. A lack of understanding of the new covenant is the reason why Christians are deceived by some preachers and the devil to beg God for what they have already been given. They keep praying to become what they are already. We need to agree with God and learn how to operate under the new everlasting covenant where God placed us by His grace.

The promises in the new covenant are better than those in the Old because the covenant is backed up and guaranteed by the Lord Jesus, the mediator of the new covenant. Jesus' precious blood seals the new covenant. The Old was basically a testament that relied upon the actions and obligations of flawed human

---

[26] Rev. Kenneth E. Hagin (specifics unknown)

beings and the sacrifices of animals to work. The Old had no power to remove the sinful nature but it was only a cover for sin. On the other hand, the New obliterated sin in its entirety and of course from the roots. Talking about the new covenant, God said,

> *<sup>16</sup>This is the covenant that I will make with them after those days, saith the Lord, I will put my laws into their hearts, and in their minds will I write them; <sup>17</sup> And their sins and iniquities will I remember no more (Hebrew 10:16-17 KJV)*

If there is a time when the understanding of the difference between the New and Old Testament and the provisions therein is important for the Body of Christ, it is now. If you listen to some Christians, you will think that God's plan for believers is to live under all the sacrifices, curses and conditions of the old covenant. Thanks be to God; we have been made free and we are free indeed and we can now walk free with our heads lifted high because of the new covenant!

In the natural, a country with a legislature has the power to repeal an old law when a new one with better provisions is enacted. The word repeal means to rescind, annul, revoke, abrogate, or make obsolete. Repealing an old law brings the new into ascendancy and supremacy over the old which is now obsolete, null and void. The same analogy is true of the New Testament. Some also wonder that if the Old Covenant is done away with, does that mean they have lost out on the blessings under the old? The answer to the question is no. God in His mercy has extricated the blessings in the Old and wrapped it all up inside the New. What that means is that being under the new covenant gives you automatic access to both the blessings under the Old plus more. I like "plus more" how about you?

Under the Old Covenant, several blessings and curses were pronounced. For someone to be blessed, he or she must do things that will prevent the curses and do a bunch of other new things to attract the blessings. Rather than doing one thousand and one things to attract the blessings today, the Bible simply states:

> *Blessed be the God and Father of our Lord Jesus Christ,*
> *who hath blessed us with all spiritual blessings in heavenly*
> *places in Christ. (Ephesians 1:3 KJV)*

How many spiritual blessings? All spiritual blessings: all that God has is available to all believers through Christ. Rather than chasing however number of blessings today, all you need to do is accept Christ and you automatically have access to all blessings (complete blessings that lack nothing). All spiritual blessings mean a lack of all curses including generational curses.

I don't mind repeating that I am not saying the Old Testament was faulty. It is God Himself; the owner of both the New and the Old that said so. Not only is the Old faulty, but God in His wisdom has replaced it with a superior, faultless, better-guaranteed covenant called the New Testament. Imagine someone who has lived in a jurisdiction where the law requires that no one is allowed to stay out beyond eleven o'clock at night. This person now travels to another jurisdiction where there are no such curfew laws which means he can now stay out for as long as he wants. If this person, due to the conditioning under the previous jurisdiction he resided, goes to the law enforcement agency to request that he be charged for breaking the law. The law enforcement people will ask him "Sir, what law have you broken?" He responds, "The law that prohibits staying out beyond eleven o'clock at night". What do you think that law enforcement will say to him? They will emphatically say to him "Sir, we don't have such curfew laws within this jurisdiction". They may also suggest to him to seek help and wonder if he is somewhat confused.

Let us assume the man insists and keeps bothering them because he strongly believes he is bound by the law of his old jurisdiction where he no longer lives; won't we all agree that something must be wrong with him and indeed recommend that he gets some kind of help?

Unfortunately, that's how some Christians think and act. Some even consider the Old Testament people like Elijah, Moses and others to have had it better than them. You can tell from listening to them that they sometimes wish they had lived in the times of Moses, Elijah, Elisha, Jeremiah and David. Friends, this is shameful! Ignorance of God's word in an area can mess you up so much that you will behave and suffer the same fate as an unbeliever. Does he not say my people are destroyed for lack of knowledge[27]?

We need to start paying attention to our thinking and our words to ensure we don't despise what Jesus did for us. He says we have been redeemed; let us say so with our mouths. Call yourself what God calls you. Tell yourself you can do whatever He says you can do. Carry yourself as the forgiven and the blessed that you are. Jesus said of all men born of a woman, none is as great as John

---

[27] Hosea 4:6

the Baptist but the least in the kingdom (what kingdom? The born-again kingdom) is greater than John the Baptist. This means that by virtue of new creation, you are greater than Moses, David, Elijah, Jeremiah and John the Baptist.

# CHAPTER 5

## Christian Growth and Living Right

To walk in our authority in Christ, we need to grow in grace and take steps toward maturity in Christ. The more of the Word you know and do, the more you grow as a believer. It is not God's plan for us to get saved and live the rest of our lives as babies who don't know wrong from right.

The writer of the book of Hebrews teaches about spiritual maturity in Hebrews 5:12-15:

> [12] *For though by this time you ought to be teachers, you need someone to teach you again the first principles of the oracles of God; and you have come to need milk and not solid food.* [13] *For everyone who partakes only of milk is unskilled in the Word of righteousness, for he is a babe.* [14] *But solid food belongs to those who are of full age, that is, those who by reason of use have their senses exercised to discern both good and evil. (Hebrews 5:12-15 NKJV)*

Notice the phrase "by reason of use" which means to practice the Word, to live the Word, to act on what we know in the Word of God. This is what Apostle James calls being a doer of the Word of God. For example, God's Word admonishes us not to be afraid. When fear comes and tries to impose itself on us, instead of falling apart and allowing our minds to go wherever the enemy suggests, we should resist the spirit of fear and enforce the peace of God given to us by our Lord Jesus. That is how we live the Word of God.

When we read the Bible and are convicted in our hearts of something the Word says, we should abandon our position that is contrary to the Word and submit to what the Word says. The more we do this, the more we grow in Christ. The only way a believer can grow in Christ is through the Word of God and fellowshipping with God through prayer. We must fellowship with the Father in prayer daily, especially praying in the spirit or tongues. According to 1 Cor 14:4 and Jude 1:20, when we pray in the spirit or tongues, we edify or build up ourselves.

God is our Father. He loves us and wants to fellowship with us. The more we fellowship in His Word and prayer, the more we grow in Him. Fellowshipping with God is reading His Word, meditating in the Word, confessing the Word and praying. We cannot spend the majority of our lives on earth in the flesh, catering for the things of the natural alone, and expect to be strong in our spirits to enjoy the rights and privileges that are ours in Christ. We also must live right and abstain from sinful and carnal living. Our boldness and confidence in God diminishes when we don't live a godly life. By living in sin, believers may open themselves up to the affliction of the devil. They will not be as bold as they should be to exercise their authority in Christ.

Remember the man healed by Jesus at the pool called Bethesda? Jesus departed very quickly from the pool after the man was healed, such that the man couldn't tell who It was that healed him. Let's read what happened when Jesus later saw the man. John 5:14:

> $^{14}$ *Afterward Jesus found him in the temple, and said to him, "See, you have been made well. Sin no more, lest a worse thing come upon you. (John 5:14 NKJV)*

Jesus said a worse thing, that is, sickness, could happen to the man if he continued in sin (or in our case, practised sin).

Curses like sicknesses and diseases are children of the devil through sin. By removing our sins, Jesus brought healing to our bodies. Wherever you see forgiveness of sin in the Bible, you will see healing. The example of this point can be found in many scriptures. For example, look at Isaiah 53:4-5, 1 Peter 2:24 and Psalm 103:1. Living right shuts the door against the enemy in a believer's life. Now, am I saying that having a problem in your life means you are living in sin? Absolutely not. You don't have to do anything for the enemy to try and attack you. Jesus said, "In the world you will have tribulation" but bless God, He didn't stop there. He said, "Be of good cheer for I have overcome the world".

# CHAPTER 6

# The Balaam Principle

As faulty as the Old Testament is in comparison to the New, the blessings pronounced under it were so superior that no curse could dislodge or neutralize it. The story of Balaam and Balak in the Bible is a good illustration of this truth. Now think about this. Even the people living under what we said was an "inferior covenant" in comparison to the New were so powerful that God said regarding them; they can not be cursed because of His superseding blessing upon their lives.

The story of Balaam and Balak[28] is one of the best examples of the power and authority conferred on the children of Israel under the Old Testament. In the biblical account of the story, the children of Israel, God's people, pitched their tents in the plains of Moab. The Moabites became afraid of them due to their largeness in number and for other reasons not mentioned. The Moabites felt distressed and overcome with fear because of the children of Israel even though we don't have an account of the children of Israel being hostile to them or planning an imminent

---

[28] Numbers 22

attack on them. The question is why were the Moabites so scared of the children of Israel?

Now, this is what the blessing does to you; it causes the devil and its agents to be scared of you. If only we will get a revelation of our authority in Christ and how we are seen in the realm of the spirit, by God, His angels, the devil and his demons, we will walk taller and care less about things like generational curses which have no hold whatsoever over us as Christians. The devil knows that we can spring the name of Jesus on him at any time; a thought that paralyzes him with unfathomable fear and dread. This is why one of his major schemes is to make you believe that you don't truly and factually possess the authority the Bible says you have in Christ so you will not use it against him. Oh! How I wish, my brothers and sisters that we will get a revelation of whom we are in Him and the authority we have been given.

Getting back to Balaam and Balak, the Moabite king thought the best way to respond to his unfounded fear of the children of Israel was to have them cursed. Balak sent for Balaam and asked him, in exchange for money and riches to curse the children of Israel before he goes up to fight against them and in his words, "peradventure I shall prevail". Notice, this heathen king who had no covenant with God understood fully well that it was the blessing of God on the children of Israel that made them prosperous and enviable. I wish some Christians could believe in the blessing of Christ in them as much as this evil king did in the blessing of the children of Israel.

God appeared to the prophet Balaam that night and asked him "Who are these people with you?" Balaam told God who they were as if God didn't already know who they were. He also told God about being asked by the king to place a curse on the children of Israel. Let us look closely at verse 12 of Numbers 22. What does it say? It says

> *And God said unto Balaam, thou shalt not go with them; thou shalt not curse the people: for they are blessed. (Numbers 22:12 NKJV)*

Friends, this is where we are going. Let's read that again, it says, **you shall not curse the people for they are blessed**. The interpretation of God's statement here is this; there is no point cursing the people for they are blessed, and curses cannot dislodge my blessing on them. Cursing them will be an exercise in futility and a detrimental mission since cursing them will bring curses upon you instead. Lord God Almighty! Can you hear that? God is saying about the people who were blessed after the order of the Old Testament that there is no point cursing them because they are blessed. God said they can not be cursed. Now, let me ask you this. On the strength of that statement by God, would you think there would have been a need to break curses off of the children of Israel also? Absolutely not! God says they can not be cursed, where then would the curse to be broken come from? Why can't they be cursed? God said, "Because they are blessed". The power of the blessing is such that a curse, generational or not, can not overcome it.

If the people under the Old Testament could be so blessed that no curse could shake them, how much more are New Testament believers? They are unmovable by the enemy. If the only reference we have in the Bible about this truth is the story of Balaam and Balak, that, to me, would have been more than enough let alone that we have this same principle and truth repeated over and over again in the New Testament as we will see later.

From what we have discussed so far, it is clear that the doctrine that proposes that generational curses could have a hold on believers is not only false but also an affront to the blood of Jesus that redeemed us and brought us into the newness of life.

Based on the Balaam principle, if I asked you the question of whether spells can be cast on a believer, I can guess what your answer would be. It will be in the negative. If blessed people can not be cursed under the Old Covenant, how possible would it be for a witch doctor to curse or cast a spell on a blessed person under the new and everlasting covenant? It is simply not possible! Let God be true and everyman a liar; if the children of Israel under the Old Covenant could not be cursed because they were blessed, I submit to you that it is simply impossible for New Testament believers to be cursed or cast a spell on. They can not be placed under any curse, generational or otherwise.

How about Galatians 3:1 where Paul asked a rhetorical question to drive his point home, asking:

> O foolish Galatians, who hath bewitched you, that ye should not obey the truth, before whose eyes Jesus Christ hath been evidently set forth, crucified among you? (Galatians 3:1 NKJV)

I can see some Bible-uneducated Christians citing this scripture as proof that it is possible that a believer can be bewitched or cast spells on. No, that will not be true.

All that Paul was trying to do here was to get the attention of the Galatian Christians in preparation for the serious discourse he was about to have with them. As we said, the question there is rhetorical at best and the obvious answer to his rhetorical question is no one bewitched or could bewitch the Galatian Christians because they have been blessed by God and hence, can't be bewitched.

Let us get back to the story. Even though prophet Balaam was forbidden by God on more than one occasion from going to Balak to carry out his unholy enterprise, motivated by money, Balaam proceeded to go anyway. His disobedience notwithstanding, the force of the blessing on the children of Israel was so powerful that an angel of the Lord had to be dispatched. The angel stood in the way of Balaam's donkey and prevented him. Balaam who at this point was spiritually dull so much that he could not sense the presence of God's holy angel, hit the donkey which left the road and went into the field because the road had been blocked by God's mighty angel. He thought it was the donkey that refused to move.

The force of the blessing not only made God allow the donkey to see into the realm of the spirit, where an angel could be seen, but it also opened the donkey's mouth so that the donkey could speak like a human. The point in this is that God, because of his blessing and the power thereof, will do whatever it takes even under the Old Covenant to protect the people upon whom such blessing rested. How far would God go to protect his blessed people? As far as it takes, I would say!

Talk about the gift of discerning spirits for a donkey. The donkey's eyes were opened to see an angel with a sword drawn. The angel blocked whichever way Balaam forced the donkey to go until the donkey ran out of options. The donkey in response to the angel finally threw herself onto the wall crushing Balaam's foot against the wall.

To bring the story to a close, the lesson to be learnt from the story of Balaam and Balak is that no one can reverse God's blessing. No one can curse him whom God had blessed. God's blessing is not only recognizable by God and his angels, but it is also recognizable by the devil and evil men. Just by observing the children of Israel, the Moabite king knew God's blessing was upon them.

Finally, if God would go to this length to demonstrate the spiritual and spectacular manifestations that we saw in this story in order to defend the blessing on His covenant people, how much more would He protect and defend us for whom the precious blood of the Lamb was shed? The same people who live under the New Covenant based on better promises. There is not and there can not be any curse upon a believer. He or she has been redeemed!

# CHAPTER 7

# The New Testament Confirmation of the Balaam Principle

Through the Balaam principle that we examined in the previous chapter, we saw how God's people who were blessed by him under the Old Covenant could not be cursed or cast a spell upon. In this chapter, we will look at some scriptures in the New Testament which were directly written to believers to see if any of them leaves room for what is called generational curses or if believers need to have such curses broken over them.

## Galatians 3:13 and the Believer

The greetings that introduced the book of Galatians clearly define Paul's targeted audience, the people he was writing to. He said "…unto the churches of Galatia:[29]" We know that church is not the building where Christians worship but it is the people who worship in the buildings. The church is God's people, the called-out ones, the believers; born-again children of the living God.

---

[29] Galatians 1:2

A basic understanding of the Bible makes us know that all the books of the Bible were written by Holy men of God who spoke as they were moved by the Holy Ghost[30]. The Epistles are letters written under the inspiration of the Holy Ghost to Christians of all ages and locations. It does not matter that they may have been directly addressed to the Romans, the Galatians, the Corinthians or the Philippians. Anything stated in the Epistles is for the believers of today.

Having resolved that, let us now examine the glorious words on the pages of Galatians 3:13. It states

> *Christ hath redeemed us from the curse of the law, being made a curse for us; for it is written, cursed is every one that hangeth on a tree: That the blessing of Abraham might come on the Gentiles through Jesus Christ; that we might receive the promise of the Spirit through faith. (Galatians 3:13 NKJV)*

To understand exactly what the words in the scripture just quoted mean, we need to read them over slowly, breaking every phrase and word into an easy-to-grasp discourse. First, it says, *Christ hath redeemed us from the curse of the law.* The word "hath" is an old English

---

[30] 2 Peter 1:21

word that means the same thing as our commonly used word "has". It connotes something that is already done and signifies that the subject in the sentence has already done all there is to be done on the subject matter. With regards to the redemption from the curse of the law which of course includes the so-called "generational curses", God in Christ already did everything there is to do and in the words of Jesus, "it is finished".

Second, the scripture also tells us how Jesus redeemed us from the curse of the law through a substitutionary work. He became a curse for us by hanging on the tree (or the cross) as it is written, cursed is anyone that hangs on the cross. Third, it tells us what the implication of Jesus' hanging on the cross is to the believers. It is, so we might receive the promise of the Spirit through faith. Brothers and sisters in Christ, it is a settled biblical truth that we have been redeemed (not going to be redeemed sometime in the near or distant future). It is not a matter of if you ever become good enough. He, Christ already redeemed us from the curse of the law.

Being born again through our acceptance of Jesus as our personal Lord and Saviour equals an automatic and absolute complete redemption from all curses, generational or otherwise. It does not matter what names the curses are given.

The great Apostle continued in verses 15-18 to prove to us that by being born again, we inherit the promise of Abraham which God made to his seed (that is Christ Jesus). He also stressed how the covenant that was confirmed before God in Abraham cannot be annulled by the law which came four hundred and thirty years later. What he is saying in clear terms is that we have not only received the blessing promised to Abraham in Christ but also that, our promised blessing in Christ can not be annulled, not by any man like Balaam, the devil or any type of curses. Our blessing and redemption are permanent and irrevocable in Christ.

The only person who can annul the blessing of God in us and upon us is God, but thanks be to God, He swore by Himself to Abraham and ratified the promise in Jesus' spotless blood. This means that annulment is impossible. It is forever! This is one of the main differentiating features between the Old and the New Covenants. The old covenant, to some extent, depends on the obedience and sacrifices of men but the new covenant is only dependent on the steadfastness and the faithfulness of Jesus who can not fail.

We don't need to hope, work or plan for it, we have it already, it is ours. Praise God! We have been redeemed from the curse of the law. Whatever they are called and in whatever format they appear, they have no hold over us anymore. If they don't have any hold on us, what sense does it make then to rid them of us by the so-called breaking them off? They have been broken and blotted out at salvation, let us stop looking all over the place for them. We don't have them anymore.

Let me make the point here that, I have never argued or contested the existence of generational curses in a nonbeliever nor do I affirm the concept. There are no chapters or verses to base its existence on in the Bible. Nonetheless, what I am asserting and hold firmly on the authority of God's word is that, generational curses have no hold on God's children and can not have a hold on them.

It makes no difference whether a curse is past, present, future, location-specific or generational. It may be binding on a nonbeliever but certainly, not on the children of God. The reason for this, as we said is that, Christ has redeemed us from all curses. The question that we are tempted to ask again is, if we have been redeemed from all curses, why then do we need generational curses broken off us? Do you mean to tell us that God's work in Christ is not complete? If the sacrifice of Jesus on the Cross, his burial and resurrection aren't sufficient to break generational curses, then what will be?

Generational curses can not be in the life of a believer, so stop chasing shadows and delving into the territory of the devil through ignorance. Stand firm in your liberty and praise God for the absolute deliverance He gave you at redemption.

God is not a man that he should lie neither is He the son of man that He should repent. Has He said, and shall he not do it or has He spoken and shall He not make it good?[31] He will not only make it good but has made it good for us in Christ.

## Colossians 2:13-15 and the Believer

The Bible says that in the mouth of two or three witnesses shall every word be established[32]. We are now going to examine other great scriptures that make a fallacy of the erroneous doctrine that says believers may have generational curses operating in their life and that require deliverance.

Colossian 2:13-15 states

> *And you, being dead in your sins and the circumcision of your flesh, hath he quickened together with him, having forgiven you all trespasses; Blotting out the handwriting*

---

[31] Numbers 23:19
[32] 2 Corinthians 13:1

*of ordinances that was against us, which was contrary to us, and took it out of the way, nailing it to his cross; and having spoiled principalities and powers, he made a show of them openly, triumphing over them in it. (Colossians 2:13-15 NKJV)*

Like the other scriptures we examined, this one is also not talking about what God might do or what we may be good enough to get someday, rather it is talking about what has already taken place. This is a reference to what Christ has already accomplished for us. It says that Christ blotted out the handwriting of ordinances that were against us, which were contrary to us. If the so-called generational curses are not against and contrary to the believers, I don't know what are. And since they are, that means He already blotted them out and nailed them to his cross.

If this scripture is true and we know it is, that means generational curses are no more on our way. They have been blotted out by our Lord Jesus. This He accomplished simultaneously when He spoiled (diminishing or destroying the value or quality of) principalities and powers making a show of them openly, triumphing over them in it. The source of all curses is sin and the devil has been dethroned, stripped of all powers and efficacy as far as a believer is concerned. The devil has no hold over us neither are his curses binding on us anymore.

To make sure you don't misunderstand me, I will like to repeat again that, I am not in any way denying the devil's dominion over the unsaved. They are his children so he can do whatever he wants with them. For us who have been born again, his hold on us has been broken. He can't lord it over us anymore. We have been made free and free indeed. We have been bought with a price and our owner is Christ who has given us all authority that belongs to Him. The devil and curses' hold over us have been broken. And if I may add, even though the unsaved are under the dominion of the devil, we believers can take advantage of God's life and work in us to get them born again so they become free like we are.

You need to believe the Bible more than we do the words of unbelieving preachers or friends who are trying to rob you of the victory we have been given over the devil, his curses and all his works through Jesus' death, burial and resurrection. Don't let anyone, no matter how famous they may be, not even an angel robs you of the blessedness you have in Him. The Bible is the word of God which must be believed, confessed, meditated upon and obeyed.

# 2 Corinthians 5:17-18 and the Believer

The next scripture we will examine with regards to the issue of the so-called generational curses is 2 Corinthians 5:17-18. It says,

> *[17]Therefore, if any man (or anyone) be in Christ, he is a new creature: old things are passed away; behold, all things are become new. [18]And all things are of God, who hath reconciled us to himself by Jesus Christ, and hath given to us the ministry of reconciliation. (2 Corinthians 5: 17-18 NKJV)*

Allow me to repeat myself here that, as with the other scriptures we examined in affirming our deliverance from and dominion over curses, this one also speaks in past tense. The Holy Ghost through the writers used past tense in these scriptures to send a clear message to us that whatever the scriptures are saying has already taken place. Not going to happen someday in the sweet by and by but has already taken place. One thing to note through these scriptures is that, the accomplishments to which we refer are not a result of something good we as individuals did but solely of what Jesus did through his immeasurable sacrifice.

The scripture we are examining starts by saying "If anyone be in Christ". The question we need to deal with before we proceed further is whether we are in Christ. If your answer to that question is yes, then you are a new creature. What does new creature mean? It means something or someone that never existed before. A new creature is not a refurbished or repaired creature. He is a brand new and of a superior nature and quality.

You are a spirit; you have a soul and you live in a physical body. What happened when you got born again was that your spirit got re-born just as Jesus explained to Nicodemus in John chapter 3. The old spirit that is corrupted by sin and the sinful nature which was inherited from Adam was removed and replaced with a brand-new spirit. Not refurbished nor reconstructed but brand new. Is it possible then for a new creature to have generational curses or any curse residing in it? Absolutely no! Where would he get curses from? Would his creator who is God put some curses on this new man to buffet and terrorize him? Absolutely not! As far as God is concerned, new means new. Old things including curses are passed away and all things have become new.

# CHAPTER 8

## A Curse is a Spiritual Substance

A curse is as much a spiritual substance just like a blessing. The implication of that is, a blessing or a curse primarily resides inside a human spirit. The question to be asked is whether both blessings and curses can reside in the same spirit at the same time. Or in other words, whether the force of righteousness, that is a blessing and a devilish force, a curse, can reside in the same spirit or upon the same person or thing at the same time. From all we have discussed so far, the answer is a definite no.

This same question was asked in a different manner in the second letter of Paul to the Corinthians. It states:

> *[14]...For what fellowship hath righteousness with unrighteousness? And what communion hath light with darkness? [15]And what concord hath Christ with Belial...[16]And what agreement hath the temple of God with idols... (2 Corinthians 6:14-16 KJV)*

The answer is obvious. The point is, curses and blessings can not coexist hence, it is either a person is blessed or cursed. You can not be blessed and cursed at the same time. We saw in Ephesians

3 that we, believers have been blessed with all spiritual blessings in heavenly places in Christ and we know that is true. If that is true, then, of a necessity a believer will not have generational curses or any other curse in or on him or her.

The Holy Ghost resides in you, not the devil nor his curses, generational or not. As we saw earlier,

> *[17]Therefore if any man be in Christ, he is a new creature: old things are passed away; behold, all things have become new. [18]And all things are of God, who hath reconciled us to himself by Jesus Christ and hath given to us the ministry of reconciliation (2 Corinthians 5: 17-18 KJV)*

All things that become new for the new creation are of God and since curses can not be of God, then, none of the "all things" will include generational curses. Also, for this new creation, old things are passed away and all things have become new. Those new things are of God. The Holy Ghost is in that new creature just as blessing is in that new creature. The devil, generational curses or any other curse can not reside in him. If there were generational curses in a believer's lineage before he got born again, that lineage changed after he got born again. He lost the old depraved, dead spirit to get a brand new one that is alive to God with the nature of God in him. Curses are part of the old things that are passed away, never to have dominion over the new creature anymore.

The cursed nature we inherited from Adam through his fall and the dominion the devil used to have over our spirits are gone. 'New' means no curse, no sickness, no disease, no poverty, lack or untimely death. No generational curses but blessing, glory, honour, anointing and sufficiency.

Had the Apostle stopped at "behold all things are become new", that would have been good enough but bless God, he went further to say, "and all things are of God". Those things that became new are of God. If they are of God, they can't be of the devil at the same time so curses will not be part of the "all things" that became new. God doesn't have curses, the devil does. The devil is the one who came to steal, kill and destroy[33] not God. The devil is the one who carries curses with him wherever he goes not God. All that God has to give are grace, blessing, goodness, mercy, loving kindness etc.

Considering all these scriptures, is it biblical to break generational curses off a Christian? Would a new creation need curses broken off him if he has been totally freed from all curses as we saw

---

[33] John 10:10

through the numerous scriptures we examined? Why break off of someone something they do not or can not have?

Nothing other than a lack of understanding of God's word would make anyone, preacher or not engage in this business of believing that a believer could have generational curses working in their life. Stop labouring in futility and chasing shadows. Christians are free from all curses whatever they may be called, pure and simple!

In a similar manner, it will be a labour in futility to want to break curses off of a nonbeliever. There is no point in doing so because someone who is not born again lives perpetually under curses as long as the devil remains his god. Unfortunately, the unsaved has no choice in the matter. What we need to do for an unbeliever is to preach the gospel to them to let them know they don't need to be under the curse anymore if they would accept and confess Jesus.

## Stand Your Ground

After Jesus resurrected from the dead, took the keys of hell and death from the devil, let the captivity captive, and secured eternal salvation for mankind; He appeared to His disciples and said these words: *"All power is given unto me in heaven and in earth. Go you therefore, and teach all nations, baptizing them in the name of the Father, and of the Son, and of the Holy Spirit: Teaching them to observe all things whatsoever I have commanded you: and, lo, I am with you always, even unto the end of the world. Amen.'*[34]

With those words, Jesus commissioned and delegated His Almighty power; all He got from the Father through his obedience and eternal sacrifice to the early Christians and other Christians that will follow. He said, "All power is given unto me in heaven and in earth." Not a few powers; all power or all authority and because He will not need the power in heaven, He delegated it to His body which is upon the earth that is you and me. We need the power to function here on the earth and thank God, we have it.

Now, it is important for me to state very clearly here that the power was not given to the Body of Christ so we can overcome the devil. Jesus already overcame the devil for us. This is why the Bible records "In all these things we are more than conquerors through him that loved us"[35] . We are not going to conquer; we already are more than a conqueror. See, all that we are asked to do is protect our territory, to occupy till He comes and to refuse

---

[34] Mathews 18:18-20

[35] Romans 8:37

to let the thief, the devil take from us what He paid such a heavy price to secure for us.

Under the Old Testament, God promised His covenant people Israel that he would rebuke the devourer (or the devil) for their sake if they would obey Him[36]. On the contrary, in the New Testament God instructs believers to rebuke the devil because they now have the power and authority that was not previously available to them. There is not one scripture in the New Testament where God promises to rebuke the devil for believers, but writers of the New Testament like Paul, Peter and James all admonish believers to resist and rebuke the devil.

Apostle Paul said, "lest Satan should get an advantage of us: for we are not ignorant of his devices.[37]" Another translation says "in order that Satan might not outwit us. For we are not unaware of his schemes.[38]" We should know God's word and use it, so the devil doesn't outwit us or have one over us nor gain an upper hand. The Bible is the light that reveals. If we will listen to God, He will reveal the devil's scheme to us so we can remain in our position of dominion over him – standing our ground.

---

[36] Malachi 3: 11
[37] 2 Corinthians 2:11
[38] New International Version (1984)

Apostle Peter said "…whom resist steadfast in the faith…[39]" How do we resist him? We resist him by being steadfast in the faith. We maintain our ground and secure our God-given territory. That means if we see anything around us that looks like the curse, generational or not; we unleash the mighty name of Jesus on it. We say no, we have been redeemed from the curse, the blessing resides in us, and we don't allow curses of any kind or any symptoms that look like them to hang around us.

The apostle James on his part said *"Submit yourself therefore to God. Resist the devil, and he will flee from you."[40]* Notice it didn't say submit yourself to the experiences of your favourite preacher or friends. No, it says to submit to God. You submit to God when you submit to His word. Submitting to His word means agreeing with Him, believing what the word says, and saying only what the word affirms.

What the writers of the New Testament inspired by the Holy Spirit were admonishing us to do in essence is to stand our ground. When the devil shows up, through unbelief and doubt, poverty, sickness and disease, and any type of curses; we are to run him out and run him off in the name of Jesus. If for whatever

---

[39] 1 Peter 5:8-9
[40] James 4:7

reason we let him run roughshod over us and refuse to use our authority or say no to him, even though he doesn't have any power over us anymore, we may find ourselves living under curse-like symptoms and occurrences that are below the standard of abundance that Christ gave us.

The devil is a liar and the father of lies[41] who has tendencies to masquerade as an angel of light[42]. The good news is he is only able to take advantage of Christians to the extent that the Christian accepts his lies and buys into his deceit.  It is not uncommon for the devil, in his deceit, to create symptoms that make it look like there are curses in your life. If you would bow to it and choose not to resist the devil and his lies and rebuke him in Jesus' name, he will run your life. As we mentioned earlier, God will not reject or resist the devil for you, you must do it for yourself. You have authority over him. Use it.

---

[41] John 8:44

[42] 2 Corinthians 11:14 (International Standard Version (2008))

# CHAPTER 9

## Dealing with Genetic Predisposition

My thoughts in this book will not be complete without dealing with the issue of genetic predisposition. What believers sometimes call generational curses is what can best be described as genetic predisposition.

In the article published in MedicinePlus[43] a genetic predisposition which is sometimes called genetic susceptibility is defined as "an increased likelihood of developing a particular disease based on a person's genetic makeup." The article continues to say that "a genetic predisposition results from specific genetic variations that are often inherited from a parent. These genetic changes contribute to the development of a disease but do not directly cause it. Some people with a predisposing genetic variation will never get the disease while others will, even in the same family."

Some believers mistake this natural phenomenon for a generational curse. As already discussed, a generational curse is a

---

[43] What does it mean to have a genetic predisposition to a disease? MedlinePlus Genetics (https://medlineplus.gov/genetics/understanding/mutationsanddisorders/predisposition/), accessed April 2, 2024.

spiritual substance not natural. If a genetic predisposition means a generational curse, then every member of the family will develop the disease to which they are genetically predisposed. The MedicinePlus article cited above says "Some people with a predisposing genetic variation will never get the disease while others will, even in the same family".

The solution of the proponents of generational curses for the believer is to have a deliverance session to break the power of genetic predispositions to disease. This is incorrect. There is no curse of genetic predisposition to be broken. If one existed, the Bible would have mentioned it, and the Apostles would have commented on it.

We know that many health issues can be prevented by a healthy lifestyle, specifically, proper diets and regular exercise. Some diseases can also be medically resolved through early intervention. If genetic predispositions were to be a curse, no natural action would be powerful enough to resolve it.

Friends, if you have been born again, there is no generational curse in your life. *And you, being dead in your sins and the uncircumcision of your flesh, hath he quickened together with him, having forgiven you all trespasses; Blotting out the handwriting of ordinances that was against us, which was contrary to us, and took it out of the way, nailing it to his cross; And having spoiled principalities and powers, he made a shew of them openly, triumphing over them in it[44].*

It is possible for a believer to have come from a natural family where people in the family are predisposed to certain diseases such as high blood pressure, heart disease, cancers, etc. What Satan does is work on the mind of the believer to convince them that since these things run in the members of their family, they too will eventually develop it and die by it.

What we do is stand our ground in Christ and enforce our authority in the name of Jesus. You must also be serious enough to start taking the right steps in the natural, such as maintaining a proper diet, exercising, and following the instructions of your physician and other medical professionals. Some of us believers erroneously think that we don't have to do anything in the natural to live a good life. You can't consume as many sugary drinks as you desire, spend all day lounging on the couch, and still expect to maintain good health.

Not that the healing power of God is not already in your spirit but your actions in the natural or lack of it may prevent the flow

---

[44] Colossians 2:13-15

of God's healing power in your body. As you do the things you should in the natural, your mouth must continually declare the word of God. You must resist the spirit of fear and reject the right of any disease to exist in your body, genetically predisposed or not.

Another important thing to note is that God is not against medical science. God was the one who gave the wisdom to health professionals to help mankind. We will always encounter baby believers in the church who may not yet know what belongs to them, let alone exercise their right to receive and walk in what belongs to them in Christ.

We will also from time to time come across lazy believers, who don't want to do what is required to live a healthy life. Medical science therefore becomes important. The purpose of medical science to a believer is to keep you alive while you grow your faith to completely resolve any sickness the enemy may bring your way.

The laziness I am referring to is why believers develop all manner of wrong doctrines when it comes to sicknesses and diseases. They say things like, God puts that on me to teach me something or to make me humble. Friends, no good father will put sicknesses and diseases on his child to teach them something.

Now, a disobedient child may end up learning the hard way the lesson he or she refuses to learn from the words of his or her father. That is not the father's fault or will, is it? No. For example, you tell a child not to go near a hot stove. Notwithstanding several admonitions, the child was disobedient. One day when the parent wasn't looking, the child touched the hot stove and got burned. Would it be correct for the child to then say "Well, dad or mom taught me a lesson by letting me get burned?" No, that will be incorrect. The child should blame his pain on his disobedience.

Our heavenly father is so merciful that even when we get burned because of our disobedience, he still makes a way of escape for us. *Fools because of their transgression, and because of their iniquities, are afflicted. Their soul abhorreth all manner of meat, and they draw near unto the gates of death. Then they cry unto the Lord in their trouble, and he saveth them out of their distresses. He sent his word and healed them and delivered them from their destructions[45].*

God won't refuse to help us because we brought the issue upon ourselves. He is a merciful father. We call on Him, He responds and helps us.

---

[45] Psalm 107:17-20

You can also consciously refuse the right of any genetically disposed disease in the name of Jesus. You should let the devil know that even though a certain disease may run in the family, you refuse its right to bring it on you.

Some other times, it may be an issue of untimely death where the grandfather, father, and uncles die at a young age. The devil will bring the fear of untimely death to the person when getting close to that age. This type of fear or thoughts are not things to disregard. They are things to deal with in the spirit, with the authority you have been given. Rather than a believer accepting that they are suffering from generational curses, believers should recognize that the devil is attempting to shoot darts of fear into their minds that must be resisted with their authority in Christ.

Understanding these things will help us think right about situations in life and will empower us to come to the right decisions both medically and spiritually. Some believers think because they believe in divine healing they shouldn't go to the doctor or take medicine or undergo medical procedures. They will not find that in the Bible. The apostle Paul said to Timothy *"Drink no longer water but use a little wine for thy stomach's sake and thine often infirmities.*[46]" He also said to Timothy *"For bodily exercise profiteth little: but godliness is profitable unto all things, having promise of the life that now is, and of that which is to come.*[47]"

What's important is to check with the Lord and to be led by the Spirit whether to go with a treatment suggested by your physician or not. Sometimes, God may want you to get a second opinion. He may also tell you to change your doctor and go somewhere else.

Whichever way you are led, one thing is sure. You must release your faith for healing and health at all times. If you are going for a medical procedure, you should ask the Lord to guide the minds and the hands of the medical professionals who will attend to you and hasten your healing and recovery such that your physicians will be amazed at the speed of your recovery.

Am I saying the only way for a believer to get healed is through medical science? Absolutely, not! There is divine healing and health in God. We have been healed by the stripes of Jesus[48] if we

---

[46] 1 Timothy 5:23
[47] 1 Timothy 4:8
[48] 1 Peter 2:24

have been born again. We can enforce our healing and take it by faith giving glory to the Lord Jesus who is our healer!

# CHAPTER 10

## Overcoming Genetic Predisposition - My Personal Testimony

The father's side of my family can be described as genetically predisposed to high blood pressure disease. Consistent with medical science, not everybody in the family is affected by it, but most are.

I am over fifty years of age at the time of writing this book, and to the glory of God, I don't have the disease or any other disease. I went for my annual physical medicals two months ago; my family doctor was surprised that I was not on any medication nor needed one. Like Caleb in Joshua chapter 14 and verse 10, the Lord has kept me and I give Him all the glory for that!

Now, my victory over high blood pressure has not been without Satan's attempt to put the disease on me. I have had a little above-normal spike on two occasions but brought it back to normal and it has stayed that way. I remember one time I did an extended travel and had a spike upon returning home. I went to a walk-in clinic doctor who told me "Well, since it runs in your family, I guess it's your time to get it." I said no, I won't get it. I will control it with lifestyle changes.

Don't ever be afraid or be respectful of anyone that you fail to speak your faith when the enemy attacks. I don't want anyone to misunderstand me, saying, "I won't get it" is not good enough but a good place to start. Your words of faith must be backed with faith actions. We learnt from the book of James that faith without action or corresponding action is dead, being alone[49].

Before discussing what I did naturally with the blood pressure spike situation, let me mention what I did spiritually. I was led by the Holy Spirit to find scriptures that have to do with light such as the following:

> 1 John 1:5: *"This is the message which we have heard from Him and declare to you, that God is light and in Him is no darkness at all."*

> James 1:17: *"Every good gift and every perfect gift is from above, and comes down from the Father of lights, with whom there is no variation or shadow of turning."*

> John 1:1-4: *"In the beginning was the Word, and the Word was with God, and the Word was God. He*

---

[49] James 2:17

*was in the beginning with God. All things were made through Him, and without Him, nothing was made that was made. In Him was life, and the life was the light of men. And the light shines in the darkness, and the darkness did not comprehend it." (NKJV)*

From the sample scriptures above, it is clear that God is light and we are the children of light because we are children of God. We also see that it is impossible for darkness to overcome light. It is light that dispels darkness, not the other way around. I meditated on these and other scriptures, educated myself, and convinced myself of the truth of the word of God.

You see, sicknesses and diseases are from the devil and came upon mankind through sin. Since I have been forgiven of my sins and am no longer under the dominion of the devil, the devil, sicknesses, and diseases no matter what they are called don't have authority over me. They can only be in my body if I allow them and that is true for you too, if you have been born again.

I started confessing that am in the light as He is in the light hence, no work of darkness, high blood pressure or any type of pressure or sickness can operate in the light therefore, sicknesses and diseases, you have to leave my body, I don't not yield my body as an instrument of unrighteousness to sickness in Jesus name!

That you did this process once and got the victory doesn't mean Satan won't come back to try and trip you up. He will bring ideas, suggestions, and thoughts but thank God, we have the help of the Holy Spirit who strengthens us and we can resist the enemy and put him where he belongs which is under our feet.

All of that being said, it is foolish to refuse to do the natural things you ought to do in the name of faith. If you are truly in faith, you will be serious enough to do all the natural things necessary in your situation. Of course, we know some people do everything naturally and still fall victim to sicknesses and diseases. It is God's power that will keep us and protect us so our faith is important. The point am making is that your spiritual activities will not take the place of sensible natural things you ought to do and vice-versa.

A lady sent me an email a while ago, reporting that she brought her mother who was sick to a meeting where I was ministering and that I prayed for her by the laying on of hands but eventually the mother died. Among other things, she told me how the mother exercised for hours every day and also ate organic food. I sympathized with her and my heart goes to her and her family and I prayed for her and her family. The point I'm making is that doing natural things alone is not enough. Our faith must be in God and His word.

In my own experience, about seven years ago, the Lord spoke to my heart "Get moving." I understood that to mean I should start exercising. I was overweight (almost obese by medical standards) at the time. I went to join a gym, and hired a trainer, paying what to me at the time was a lot of money. By the grace of God, I kept at it and got used to exercising. Today, I exercise first thing in the morning and most days at night. I also educated myself about a proper healthy diet and started eating right.

My lifestyle has changed drastically and in a sustained manner. I have lost weight and living in good health to the glory of God, and I plan to keep it that way.

Another point to make is that some believers are too flippant with their health. They won't go for their regular checkups or take seriously what they should take seriously. If you are not disciplined enough to abstain from foods and lifestyles that are detrimental to your health, I doubt that you are serious enough to develop a strong faith for healing.

I tell people that if they don't know what is wrong with them, how would they know what to attack with their faith? The word says "*For verily I say unto you, that whosoever shall say unto this mountain, be thou removed, and be thou cast into the sea; and shall not doubt in his heart but shall believe that those things which he saith shall come to pass; he shall have whatsoever he saith*[50]. Notice the words "this mountain" used in the verse. You must know what the mountain is to be able to speak the word of faith directly to it and see it removed and cast into the sea.

You will agree with me that it is much easier to accept that there is a generational curse of high blood pressure that someone can in vain cast out of you than to focus and do all the things I have been talking about in this book. We labour to enter into the rest and that labour is the labour of meditating on the word until it becomes revelation knowledge in our spirits and acting upon what we know both spiritually and naturally.

---

[50] Mark 11:23

# CHAPTER 11

## You Have Authority in Christ

Notwithstanding the predisposition you may have been exposed to from your natural lineage or background, genetic or not, if you have been born again, you have authority over Satan and his demon spirits in the name of Jesus.

You see, the thought about genetic predisposition is used by Satan to bind a believer. It will work through your knowledge of things that run in your family to bring fear, intimidation, and stronghold into your mind thereby controlling you. You and I can say no to all of that.

We must not forget that if we have been born again, we have been delivered from the power of darkness and translated from the kingdom of darkness to that of God's dear son, Jesus, the Christ[51]. We may have come from a natural family with all manner of negative genetic dispositions such as sicknesses and diseases, but you and I in Christ Jesus have now been re-born into a new family, the family of God. In the family of God, there is no predisposition to anything negative or evil.

---

[51] Colossians 1:13

*Christ has redeemed us from the curse of the law, being made a curse for us for it is written, cursed is every one that hangs on the tree: that the blessing of Braham might come on the Gentiles through Jesus Christ: that we might receive the promise of the Spirit through faith[52].*

You see, what the enemy uses against us is our lack of knowledge of God's word concerning spiritual warfare. A good understanding of the Bible-taught spiritual warfare is to know who you are in Christ, the authority you have been given in Christ, and the spiritual supernatural weapons you have been given in Christ to live successfully. You should also know the enemy and the weapons he uses against the believer so you can out-manoeuvre him in the spirit.

When most of us believers think about the devil and demon spirits, we think from the perspective that Satan, the devil, and demon spirits have power but God's power is more than their power. while it is true that Satan has his own power, it is nothing to be compared to the power of God. Just as a house can't claim to have any power in comparison to the builder, we must know that the power of the devil is over those who have not been born again.

---

[52] Galatians 3:13-14

For you that have been born again, Satan has no power whatsoever over you. Look at how Paul by the inspiration of the Holy Spirit described it in Ephesians 2:1-6. He made it clear that you and I before we came into Christ used to be controlled by the prince of the power of the air, the spirit that works in the children of disobedience[53]. Rather than Satan or demon spirits having power over you, the New Testament teaches that a born-again believer has authority and power over Satan and demon spirits.

One of the first truths revealed by Jesus after His resurrection is our authority in the name of Jesus to cast out demons. He said in my name they that believe in Him will cast out demons. He then listed other signs that will follow the believer. However, it is interesting and instructive to note that the believing ones will cast out demons was the first sign Jesus mentioned[54].

Jesus, during His earthly ministry, when He sent out the disciples to do the works of Christ, the disciples came back to give the testimony, to their amazement, that demons were subject to them in Jesus' name. He said to them *"…. I beheld Satan as lightning fell from heaven. Behold, I give unto you power to tread on serpents and scorpions*

---

[53] Ephesians 2:1-6
[54] Mark 16:17-18

*and over all the power of the enemy: and nothing shall by any means hurt you*[55]*."*

The author of sickness, disease, infirmities, pain, poverty, lack, and everything negative in this world is the devil. Those negative genetic dispositions were orchestrated by the devil. God did not create anything bad or defective. Whenever we see any defect or disability or sickness and disease in people, we should understand those were directly or indirectly affected by the devil, not God. The apostle James made this point succinctly by the Holy Spirit.

The apostle James said *"Every good gift and every perfect gift is from above, and cometh down from the Father of lights, with whom is no variableness, neither shadow of turning*[56]. Anything contrary or that looks different from good and perfect gifts is not and cannot be from God. That is what the Bible teaches.

Satan is a liar. Jesus said so. Jesus said when he speaks, he is lying and when he lies, he is speaking his native language. He is the father of lies who has lied from the beginning. It is no surprise then that he twists things, misrepresents things, and confuses people.

---

[55] Luke 10:18-19
[56] James 1:17

Generational Curses & the Christian Believer | 99

Let me go back to what I said earlier. What the enemy uses against us is our lack of knowledge of God's word concerning spiritual warfare. A good understanding of the Bible-taught spiritual warfare is to know who you are in Christ, the authority you have been given in Christ, and the spiritual supernatural weapons you have been given in Christ to live successfully. You should also know the enemy and the weapons he uses against the believer so you can out-manoeuvre him in the spirit.

Spiritual warfare is not commanding the demons over a city to fall or for the devil to die and all of that. The Bible doesn't teach any of these things just as the Bible never taught the New Testament believer to break generational curses simply because a born-again believer in the eyes of God does not have any curses, generational or not. He or she has as one of my pastor friends says, "generational blessings," praise God.

You and I must know who we are in Christ. We are the righteousness of God in Christ Jesus. We are children of God. We are the Body of Christ and members in particular. We are not wimpy or weak, we are strong, the word of God abides in us, and have overcome the wicked one[57]. The Bible also teaches that "*Ye*

---

[57] 1 John 2:14

*are of God, little children, and have overcome them: because greater is he that is in you than he that is in the world.*"[58]

Who is in you? The mighty Holy Spirit. The greatest power-giver in the universe. Who is he that is in the world? Satan, the devil, the enemy, demon spirits. The Bible says that He that is in us is greater than he that is in the world, praise God. We must accept that as the truth and believe it.

As I mentioned, Satan no longer has authority over someone who has been born again. Consequently, unlike Hollywood movies, Satan doesn't come with two horns and pitchforks. The way he comes to believers today is the exact way he came to Jesus when he tempted him in the wilderness. He comes with thoughts and imaginations which may later become a stronghold if the believer fails or delays to use his or her authority to stop him.

> 2nd Corinthians 10:3-6: (NKJV) For *though we walk in the flesh, we do not war after the flesh: (For the weapons of our warfare are not carnal, but mighty through God to the pulling down of strong holds;) Casting down imaginations, and every high thing that exalteth itself against the knowledge of God and bringing*

---

[58] 1 John 4:4

*into captivity every thought to the obedience of Christ;*
*And having in a readiness to revenge all disobedience,*
*when your obedience is fulfilled.*

This passage of scripture informs us of the weapons used by the devil against us and the weapons we have to use against him so we can handle him and put him in his place when he shows up to prevent being defeated by him. The passage started by letting us know that the weapons of our warfare are not carnal. Not natural or fleshy which means they are supernatural and divine. They are mighty through God.

# CHAPTER 12

## You Will Have What You Say

Most Christians bring about the effect of curses in their lives by what they say. The devil knows that he doesn't have any power over you if you have been born again but he also knows that if he can deceive you into not being mindful of what you say, he can turn the most powerful tool that God gave you; your mouth, to a weapon against yourself.

The primary principle in Mark 11:23 is that a believer can have what he or she says. This is true whether you are saying the word of God that is full of power and ability; or doubt and unbelief which has the potential to wreak havoc in your life. The fact that you are willing to believe in and submit yourself to someone to break generational curses off you even though you are a Christian who has been redeemed from the curse of the law is evidence that you do not understand your authority in Christ neither are you in the habit of speaking God's word out of your mouth. It is also evidence that you are living in fear, doubt, and unbelief.

Let us see through an illustration how a believer can entrap himself and subject himself to curse-like effects or symptoms through the words of his mouth. An example of what they call "generational curses" is untimely death. Let us assume that a grandfather died at the age of sixty and his son at fifty. The grandson, who is born again and now in his thirties and ignorant about God's word believes the lie of the devil that since his grandfather died at sixty and his dad at fifty that means there is some generational curse working in their family which may make him not live to see his fiftieth birthday.

Instead of taking authority over that thought of untimely death, rebuking the devil, and declaring with his mouth what the Bible says about him fulfilling the numbers of his days and God satisfying him with long life; he buys into the lie of generational curses and doesn't know much about his authority in Christ. What does he do? He starts speaking death with his mouth telling himself and later others that he may not see his fiftieth birthday. If he keeps saying this long enough, he will believe it and the devil will work to make that happen for him which means he has what he said. You may ask, what if he got someone to break the curse of untimely death off him? The point is he doesn't have a curse of untimely death because he is a believer. What needs to be broken off him if that is possible; is his froward mouth and his un-renewed mind which overwhelms and brings about death, doubts, and unbelief.

Let's assume for a moment that a type of curse runs upon your family lineage, the day you got born again, you got redeemed from all curses – known and unknown. Your lineage changes to that of Jesus of Nazareth. Remember we said that a curse is a spiritual substance which means it primarily will reside in the human spirit. Your spirit which has been re-born can't have death in it.

I remember listening to a message on CD by a popular minister in the United States who spoke about how their family suffers from a heart condition that causes them to become somewhat disabled by the time they are in their forties.  Upon realizing this and knowing that he had been redeemed from the curse of the law, he started saying what he believed through his mouth. He said that he has been redeemed from a heart condition, its symptoms, and anything that looks like it. He says his heart is strong and healthy and the number of his days God will fulfil.

He said whenever he and his wife go to his family members, his father, and brother, they will say things like "You need to take it easy son, you do too much travel and don't get enough rest, remember the heart condition situation." He says his wife will respond each time by saying "he is fine, he will never have a heart condition, his heart is strong; leave him alone."  He was sixty at the time he preached the message and he testified that he has never had any symptoms or any issues with his heart. His heart is strong and healthy by what he says with his mouth.

If thoughts of not living your life out or of an incurable disease or something serious like that start coming to your mind, it is not because there is a curse on your life, it is the devil throwing his scary darts at you to see if you will fall for his lies. Your response to that should be this: find scriptures that promise you long life, healing, health, and a prosperous life and meditate on them so your mind is renewed in the area. A renewed mind will cause your mouth to speak the words your mind has been renewed to.

The process of mind renewal will in no time begin to change the way you see yourself. You will begin to see yourself grow older than anyone ever did in your natural family. Your imagination also will be affected by God's word that you are meditating on and speaking out of your mouth. Soon, you will begin to see yourself through the eyes of your spirit and grow old enough to attend your grandchildren's graduation ceremony. You will start planning for a future that is longer than fifty, sixty, seventy, and eighty years of age. The power of God will work in your life until you are satisfied with a good long life.

If you go around saying your grandpa died at fifty, your uncle died at fifty-two, your dad died at fifty-five, no one lives to be sixty in your family and you are not likely going to live to be sixty; I am sorry to break the news to you, you will have what you say. If by a special miracle of God, you live to see your sixtieth birthday, it may not be with many years past that.

We see people around us who live in fear of death where one disease or another is concerned. Some whose mother or family member died of breast, colon, or other types of cancer have a natural tendency to live in fear of these diseases. You need to realize that any type of fear is of the devil. Fear is not from God. As it did to Job, fear that is left unchecked will cause havoc in the life of a believer. Job said, *"For the thing which I greatly feared has come upon me, and that which I was afraid of has come unto me."*[59] We need to resist the devil in this area of fear as well.

> Hebrews 2:15 (NKJV) says *"Since then the children are partakers of flesh and blood, he also himself likewise took part of the same; that through death he might destroy him that had the power of death, that is, the devil;*

---

[59] Job 3:25

*And deliver them who through fear of death were all their lifetime subject to bondage."[60]*

The fear of death subjects one to bondage. There is no reason why a child of God needs to live under any kind of bondage. Rather than feeling hopeless and pronouncing yourself as someone upon whom there are generational curses, you need to lay your hands on your head and command whatever sickness and disease in your body to die and disappear because you are the redeemed of the Lord and those diseases will obey you.

Whenever the devil reminds you of diseases which may have killed your loved ones, rebuke him and say to him you are not afraid because God has not given you the spirit of fear. Tell him that God has redeemed your life from destruction and you will not die but live to declare the works of God. Let him know that your case is different, and no disease will come on you or kill you because greater is He that is in you than those diseases. Tell him that the Bible says by His stripes you were healed and that no weapon that is formed or fashioned against you shall prosper. The devil doesn't like a believer who speaks in this manner. He will

---

[60] Hebrews 2:14-15

flee from you, and you will live a victorious life void of diseases, calamities, untimely death, and anything the devil can bring.

Remember the children of Israel who said they were not able to take the land even though God told them He had given the land to them[61]? God had no choice but to agree with them and their words caused them to be destroyed in the wilderness. Caleb and Joshua on the other hand, whom God described as having another spirit, the spirit of faith; released the word of faith through their mouths and said what God said. They said that they were more than able to take the land; they made it and took the land even though they were well advanced in age.

It bears repeating that noticing a symptom of generational curses in your life does not mean you are under a curse[62]. You hand over power in your life to what you believe. You need to make up your mind and stop believing in the power of generational curses to control your life and your future. The way you do this is by asserting your righteous nature in Christ. When you do, you will live free and strong of all symptoms and fulfill the number of your

---

[61] Number 14:24

[62] Pastor Nancy Dufresne in a message at POLC Mississauga ON, Sept 26, 2012

days. This, friends, is the fight of faith we have been called to fight; protecting our God-given territory.

You can not set your words against God's word and expect to enjoy His blessings. Setting yourself against God's word opens the door to the devil to wreak havoc and ruin your life. Say the right things. Things like, I have been redeemed from the curse of the law. I am redeemed from untimely death. The number of my days God will fulfill. With a long life, He satisfies me and shows me His salvation. I am not afraid of death for I have been redeemed from it. I will live and not die to declare the works of God. I will live out my years in prosperity and days in pleasure!

You are maintaining your ground when you talk that way. You are agreeing with God. You are submitting to Him. You are putting His protective overcoming angels to work for you. You are saying what He says and since He is not a man that would lie, His word will not return to Him void. You will enjoy the fruits of your words.

# CHAPTER 13

## The Choice is Yours

One of the greatest gifts given to mankind by God is the power of choice. God respects and will protect the choices we make. Even though His perfect desire and will is for us to line our will up with His word, if we choose not to do so, He will not force us. He wants us to submit ourselves to His will voluntarily. He is a good God who will not violate our will or make us do His will whether we like it or not.

The good news is that we do know His will because His will is revealed in His word. If all you have ever heard about His word are the few scriptures discussed in this book, you know more than enough to live victorious upon the earth. All that is left for you to do is to choose whether you will believe God's word and trust Him or continue to be ignorant and run with wrong teachings which have been problematic to our believing and faith life thus far. As your brother in the Lord, I want to admonish you to please go with God's word. His will for you is to live a life free of all curses. Receive it and live the abundant life He has provided for you.

All the handwriting of ordinances that were against you and contrary to you has been blotted out. He has redeemed you from the curse of the law and has made you a new creature in Christ. Old things are passed away in your life and all things have become new. Let us all choose to be on God's side. Dare to call yourself what He calls you in His word and use the authority He secured for you over the enemy.

Moses, the man of God under the Old Covenant provided God's people, the children of Israel, with an option between the curse and the blessing[63]. He admonished them to choose life that both they and their children may live. Ladies and gentlemen, I have news for you. Jesus, through His sacrifice on the cross and resurrection took the curse option away hence the only option available to believers today is blessing.

Remain and abound in your covenant blessing and don't allow the devil to lord his curses over you through ignorance or by accepting that even though you are a believer, you still have some curses looming over your life which requires breaking. That is not true. You have been made free so stand fast therefore in the liberty wherewith Christ hath made you free and be not entangled

---

[63] Deuteronomy 30:19

again with the yoke of bondage[64]. This doctrine of breaking curses off a believer is a yoke of bondage. Refuse to be entangled by it. Remain free in Him and give thanks continually for what He has done for you. Forget not all His benefits!

---

[64] Galatians 5:1`

# About the Author

Reverend Busuyi Aroso is an anointed minister of the Gospel who preaches and teaches the Word of God with passion, clarity, and simplicity. His down-to-earth and funny demeanour style of preaching endear him to believers in the Body of Christ. He also flows in the gifts of the Spirit as the Spirit wills for the edification of the Body of Christ.

His life pursuit is to see believers gain an understanding of what they have been given in Christ so that they can live successfully on earth.

Rev. Aroso is the president of Faith Contenders Ministries (FCM) Canada, the ministry he founded with his wife in September, 2012. He is also the president of Faith Contenders Ministries (FCM), USA and Contenders Gospel Church, Nigeria.

Among the outreaches of FCM is a radio broadcast ministry, "An Audience with the King", which currently airs on 41 radio stations in the US in more than 17 states, 5 stations across Canada and 6 stations in Nigeria.

He holds bi-monthly in-person Faith Seminars in the Greater Toronto Area of Canada and internationally. He has held Faith Seminars in Canada, the US, the UK and Nigeria. His weekly live broadcast, "An Audience with the King Online", broadcasts on Facebook and YouTube Live every Monday at 6 pm EST. Busuyi also speaks at local churches, seminars and conferences, both locally and internationally. In obedience to the leading of the Lord, he and his wife have just started Faith Contenders Church in addition to other outreaches of the ministry. He and his wife, Yomi, have been happily married for 27 years and blessed with adult twin daughters.

To reach him, please visit www.faithcontenders.org and or send an email to info@faithcontenders.org.

Printed in Great Britain
by Amazon

50616052R00069